brad pattison unleashed

BRAD PATTISON

BRAD PATTISON

UNLEASHED

A Dog's-Eye View of Life with Humans

Vintage Canada

VINTAGE CANADA EDITION, 2010

Copyright © 2010 Brad Pattison

Published in Canada by Vintage Canada, a division of Random House of Canada Limited, Toronto, in 2010. Originally published in hardcover in Canada by Random House Canada, a division of Random House of Canada Limited, in 2010. Distributed by Random House of Canada Limited.

Vintage Canada with colophon is a registered trademark.

www.randomhouse.ca

Library and Archives Canada Cataloguing in Publication

Pattison, Brad
    Brad Pattison unleashed : a dog's-eye view of life with humans / Brad Pattison.

Includes index.

ISBN 978-0-307-35775-5

    1. Dogs—Training. I. Title.

SF431.P363 2010   636.7'0887   C2010-903821-5

Book design by Terri Nimmo

Printed and bound in the United States of America

10 9 8 7 6 5 4 3 2 1

To my father Ken Pattison;
my brothers Kevin and Kurtis Pattison;
and Kia, Dez and Max,
who have been the most inspirational teachers and dog
buddies one could ever hope for.

CONTENTS

Acknowledgments

Special thanks go to both my two-legged and my four-legged clients for putting their faith in my training methods and philosophies. The process of building a healthy human-dog relationship can be incredibly demanding—pushing boundaries, comfort levels, patience and sometimes sanity. But I hope you know that my faith in *you* comes from a place of the utmost respect for your strengths and unique personalities and a deep appreciation of the power of a great interspecies bond. You've taught me so many things, and your prints are all over this book, whether through intimate first-person stories or the various techniques and ideas I've developed.

Thanks also to the many dog trainers who have graduated from my dog-training school. I draw great strength from you—knowing that you're out there, striving to raise the bar on dog training, helping challenge negative trends and backward conventions and motivating clients to strive for their personal bests. I'm tempted to thank the doubters and naysayers as well. I've learned a lot about what to avoid by studying conventional trainers' methods and the personalities that shape some of their approaches to dog training. But many of these people downplay, ignore or altogether dismiss the unique smarts, skills and needs of dogs, and I don't think anyone deserves thanks for that. Instead, my thanks go out to the dogs and people who have endured such negative attitudes and prevailed to prove these people wrong.

Thanks go, as well, to everyone at Random House—most especially Anne Collins, my editor and publisher extraordinaire, whose seemingly tireless curiosity and open-mindedness helped this book take shape.

To my writing collaborator—self-described "cat person" Danielle Egan—thanks for the many great conversations, for organizing and translating my actions-speak-louder methods into words and for discovering your own inner dog in the process.

Special thanks to my dad, Ken Pattison; my brothers, Kevin and Kurt; and my dogs Kia, Dez and Max. All have helped me appreciate the importance of challenging the status quo, and they've taught me that sometimes you have to make mistakes and take some hard knocks and endure pain and loss in order to succeed. Having such strong roots in my life keeps me humble, grounded and inspired to learn more. The dogs have passed away, but their special qualities survive in the teachings they gave to me and to other dogs.

You've Come a Long Way, Doggy

I have so many phenomenal dogs in my life. My oldest dog has been around for thirty million years! Well, it's not actually a dog; it's a prehistoric, canine skull. I keep it at my training centre as a reminder that dogs thrived all over the world long before we rolled out the welcome mat for them. They haven't changed much since that ancient doggy's day. They still need to be part of a highly organized and efficient pack. They still need to walk and run around, checking out the local "daily news" by sniffing the territory and adding their own bylines to the mix. They still play, bond socially and seek out mental stimulation and new environments. And they still like to use their impressive skills for hunting, even though we now provide most of their food.

The only thing that has changed a bit along the way is the fur packaging. Primitive canids were sleek and shorthaired, and they looked more like scavenging rodents or hyenas than dogs by our pampered-pooch standards. But our ancestors didn't look so hot back then either, swinging from trees and dragging their knuckles on the ground.

Our environment has morphed radically since then—especially in the last few hundred years—and it's changing every day. We've come a long way in many respects, and dogs have evolved with us in order to suit our changing needs and desires. In recent centuries, dogs have been bred to have specific jobs, such as providing human protection and helping us hunt, herd or travel by sled. Chances are, those dogs gave us back many of the amazing perks we enjoy today—like affection, companionship, loyalty and trust. Today's domestic dog no longer works but spends most of the day languishing at home, waiting for us to return and throw her a bone or two in the form of fresh air, exercise, socialization and play. We too often ignore the simple fact that dogs have very basic, ancient needs. We also neglect to give them the chance to use their incredible range of skills and smarts. Many owners push the dog envelope by forcing their four-legged buddies to act as surrogate human partner, stuffed animal and lap warmer all rolled into one living, breathing fur coat. In other words, we're forcing our dogs to live dull, stressful and stifling lives.

When I opened up my first dog daycare facility eighteen years ago and started focusing my attention on the canine set, I quickly realized that when it comes to our relationships with our four-legged best friends, we've become downright addlebrained compared to our ancestors. Many owners and trainers ignore dogs' basic needs and skills, which makes it very difficult to educate them to live safely and contentedly in our modern human packs, and this often results in negative dog behaviours that can be hard to fix and downright dangerous for both species.

Don't get me wrong, I'm not a Luddite pining away for some simpler life-gone-by. I'm practically stapled to my Smackberry, which delivers a steady stream of emails from dog owners who've found my website online and are looking for advice. I'm a frequent flyer and I travel all over the globe, hosting seminars, doing private and group dog-training sessions and teaching other dog trainers my techniques. I make use of TV, radio and the Internet to send my views and methods to homes around the world, and my techniques have been developed to suit our fast-paced, time-strapped lives. Some of you might know me from my reality TV series, where I coach people who are trying to fix their dysfunctional dog-human relations. For the show, I use surveillance cameras so my clients can't use the excuse that the dog ate their homework.

I am typically called in to homes to fix owners' mucked-up dogs, but more often than not, it's the *people* who are in the greatest need of training—and it's definitely more challenging to do that. Doggy problems are often symptoms of dysfunctional two-legged dilemmas, like relationship breakdowns within families and many other complex human issues that are often mistakenly heaped onto our dogs' furry backs. Implementing an effective dog-training program sometimes means walking into a minefield of emotions, digging up and sifting through sensitive and personal human issues. Many people expect a doggy quick-fix, so it can be a rude awakening to have a dog trainer point out that the buck stops with them.

The most successful dog owners are willing to make a commitment to their pets and recognize that the payoffs are enormous for both species. I've been around dogs my entire life, and the beauty of a great human-dog relationship still continually blows me away, whether it's mine or that of a complete stranger. When I see a person who's in sync with their dog, I feel even more motivated to work on those "last-resort" cases.

Before you start picturing me up on a soapbox, pitching some cultish Order of the Dog movement, I should clarify that I get the biggest buzz of all when I see synchronicity playing out in the most basic, everyday activities, like the twenty-minute, pre-work dog-walking ritual. I saw one pair the other day, strolling along a busy street in downtown Vancouver. The dog was off-leash, but he didn't run ahead or bolt into the street. And the woman who owned him gave him enough time to pick up the daily news—on a fire hydrant, on a pole. Eventually, the pooch added his own quick byline and moved on. Meanwhile, his owner didn't speed-walk ahead and yell, "Come on!" at him, and he didn't freak out and start barking when she paused to send a text message.

Even when she quickly ducked inside a café, he sat patiently by the door, people watching, only occasionally glancing inside to check on her progress. In fact, the two rarely acknowledged each other at all—at least not in an obvious way. When the owner came out of the café, she gave the dog a brief rub behind the ear, but otherwise, there was no touching, and not a single word passed between them. Most people probably wouldn't have noticed them at all. But it was obvious to me that these two have a wickedly good relationship, based on mutual trust and respect: the dog could roam around off-leash, even on a busy downtown street, and his owner could provide her dog with his fix of sights, smells and socialization without worrying that he'd bolt into the street. Seeing interactions like that continually fuels my belief that with a little effort and some basic training skills that rely on the strengths and needs of both species, *everyone* can have a special bond with their dog.

By comparison, other modern interspecies trends add up to what seems like a gong show to me—dogs shackled in prong collars like dungeon prisoners on a day pass, yanking their owners around; two-legged meltdowns when dogs ignore their owners' desperate pleas for cooperation at dog parks; Barbie Dogs in mink coats and jewelled collars being carried around like fashion accessories and status symbols; gourmet doggy bakeries and luxury pet boutiques; cavernous doggy stores hawking useless, and sometimes dangerous, pet lifestyle products; the yearly doggy supermodel fashion shows that turn dog breeds into disposable trends; and the so-called "positive reinforcement" treat-training nonsense that has turned people into doggy vending machines and dogs into potentially lethal weapons.

I know there are much better ways to cultivate a great life with our dogs—one that nurtures both species. Although it's imperative to adapt training to our modern lives, my techniques have also evolved not only from noticing the ways dogs interact with dogs at dog parks, at my dog daycare facilities and in my group training sessions but also by observing wolves while hiking in the mountains and by spending years watching urban coyotes in Calgary. The many exercises I'll describe in this book fuse the hard-wired skills and needs of dogs with the needs and desires of humans.

In our fast-paced, techno-centric modern world, a well-balanced dog can enrich our lives in so many ways—by feeding *our* needs for exercise, play and loyal and trustworthy companionship. Both species desire a purpose in life, and I know that if we have dogs who *want* to be in our lives, we'll also have a life worth sharing with our dogs.

Busting the Myths

In this book, I'll bust the most common myths and misconceptions we have about dogs and dog training—particularly the ways we perceive, misdiagnose and mistreat "normal" or "problem" dog behaviours. Some of the myths that we project onto our dogs, sometimes long before we've even met them, come from our own fairy-tale ideals. We have every good intention for our four-legged friends, but sometimes the methods are utterly lost in translation. Some myths have been pushed on us by other dog trainers who might be able to lure our dogs to obey in a sterile warehouse classroom. But as soon as dog and owner are out in the real world, with all of its tantalizing distractions, those lessons count for nothing—and more often than not, they compound dogs' problem behaviours.

I think it's high time that we start respecting and celebrating dogs' long-standing needs, as well as their innate skills and abilities. Dogs are much smarter than many people believe. They try so hard to be team players in our complex human culture—and that's one of the reasons we love them so much! But dogs also misunderstand our attempts at teaching them how to become well-adjusted dog citizens, which leaves both species befuddled. In order to become good teachers and caregivers, why not start taking a dog's-eye view of the world? Our canine companions make great attempts to be heard and understood every day—in a language that is actually very easy to learn—once you understand the handful of terms that sum up your pooch's basic needs. I speak fluent dog primarily through my actions: by being the pack leader *at all times*, teaching my dogs and my dog clients the human rules of conduct so both can navigate safely in our world. I give the dogs a mix of experiences by taking them for lots of walks and hikes, providing all kinds of mental stimulation, playing with them and letting them socialize with other dogs, all the while being attentive to their body language and behaviour so I can gauge their changing moods. I also consider how my own actions and behaviours might negatively impact their lives, and I trust them to show *me* their innate skills and talents so their unique personalities can shine through.

Unfortunately, when people choose to ignore their dog's basic needs, they wreak a lot of havoc, even to the point of causing their pet to suffer greatly or even lose its life. I'm sick of seeing dogs being dumped, sent to shelters and euthanized. The overwhelming majority of these forgotten pups could have been great pets, and too often the missing ingredient was sensible guidance from their human caregivers. Only humans can make the changes needed to set their dogs up for successful cohabitation.

Turning over a New Leash

My goal in writing this book is not to scare you into submitting to my dog-training methods and ideas. It's to help you enrich your relationship with your dog and suggest ways for you to discover and cultivate characteristics and skills you've never seen in your dog before. I'm going to share some of my experiences with the many phenomenal dogs

I've come to know well over my lifetime and some of the dogs I've had the pleasure of working with as a trainer. If you watch my TV show, *At the End of My Leash*, you will already have met many of these star dogs—like Rocky, Rudy, Jackson and Bisco. All of them were really messed up when I met them, but as you'll find out, with hard work, perseverance, consistency and guidance, they became stellar dog citizens. I hope their stories help give you the incentive to follow the training guidelines in this book so you can strengthen your bond with your dog.

My Life with Dogs

First, I want to introduce you to the dogs who have enriched my life and give you some background on how I developed the training methods that some people call unconventional and others call bleeping crazy—until they see how well these techniques work (though even then, some still think I'm crazy).

It all started when a bright light came down from the sky—just kidding. Talk about mythologizing, right? That couldn't be further from the truth. I didn't have any light-bulb, it's-my-destiny-to-be-a-dog-trainer moment. I actually came to this work through a long process that started with having awesome dogs around me from early childhood and on. And, no, wolves didn't raise me. In fact, I had great two-legged mentors, teachers and friends. A few very difficult events also had dramatic impact, changing the course of my life—ultimately for the better. But I don't believe that any-thing happens overnight. In my mind, you have to make a conscious effort to strive for success—whatever that means to you—and it takes a lot of work, study, careful observation, curiosity and a strong desire to challenge the status quo.

I have only hazy memories of the first two dog members of the Pattison family: a boxer named Duke, followed by a Schipperke named Aldo. I asked my dad, Ken, why he wanted to have dogs in the family, and he said that because he was born and raised on a farm where there were working dogs (in Shaunavon, Saskatchewan), he wanted us kids to have animals in our lives too. For farmers and ranchers, training dogs is simple: give them water, kibble and a job. To these folks, it seems like a no-brainer that dogs are dogs and people are people and that it's important and beneficial to fulfill the needs of both species by giving them shelter, food and a great variety of physical and mental stimulation—ultimately, a purpose in life.

I saw with my own eyes how a dog thrives in that kind of environment when we moved to a large property in the country and got three horses and Queenie, a Heinz 57, mixed-breed dog. That dog was so cool and so smart. She was a buddy who did all the Tom Sawyer–Huck Finn-type things with me and my older brothers, Kevin and Kurt, exploring things with us everywhere, looking for frogs and porcupines, going cross-country skiing with us, taking the horses four miles to the corner store to buy candy bars, running out to greet us every day when the yellow bus dropped us off after school.

By comparison, school was a bit like prison for me. I didn't take to learning in such a sterile environment. My dad used to say, "Just because someone has been doing the same thing day in and day out doesn't mean that his or her way is the best way." He trusted and encouraged me to believe that if something didn't make sense, I should challenge it. Granted, that philosophy got me into a bit of trouble at school, but it became especially helpful when I started observing dog trainers.

My first dog lesson actually came from my brother Kevin. I was visiting my parents with my dog Kia, a heeler-shepherd cross. I was bragging about how I had taught Kia to sit down obediently as soon as she set foot on the front doormat. Kevin wasn't impressed. "Be surprised when your dog does something wrong," he said, "not when your dog does something right." I guess my bro was teaching me a lesson in humility, but the message stuck: we should have positive expectations for our dogs and trust that they can develop many skills.

I was an adult by then, living back in Calgary, with my own landscaping company and a day job selling medical supplies. I had to travel a lot, and I often took Kia with me— we sneaked into a lot of hotels and never got caught. (You could smoke in hotels, but you couldn't take in a dog?) Kia had to be really well behaved to do that, and I always made a game of it, trusting that she could pull off going in unnoticed, which she did. Kia, like Queenie, was always in the mix of my life. We had stupid amounts of fun together.

My second dog-training experience was at a group training session. It took place in a big, drafty, sterile warehouse, so there were none of the usual sensory elements that tantalize and distract dogs—like new smells, squirrels rustling in the trees or car traffic. Teaching a dog how to acquire even basic skills like "sit" and "stay" in that environment didn't seem to be of any use in the real world. Worse, the dog trainer was more into humiliating dogs than helping them learn. He was undermining and belligerent, offering nothing but put-down after put-down, bullying the dogs into submission.

Nice, huh? I would never, ever abuse a dog physically, and it made no sense to me that anybody, whatever the species, could actually learn anything through physical or verbal abuse. I've since learned that there are many trainers out there who just kick the crap out of dogs, both literally and figuratively. That training session was my first eye opener, and it helped plant a seed that would later bear a lot of fruit.

But I had to suffer some heartache first. I got home from work one day and went to get Kia from the backyard. She was gone, but her collar was lying on the grass. That was a terrible sign. I would rather have believed that she'd somehow got out of the yard and run off. Anyway, I had to try to find her. I put posters up everywhere and went to nearby shelters every day. I searched for months—I still look for her sometimes.

A Big Scoop

That dark period was a catalyst for me to start thinking that there must be a better way to take care of our dogs while we're at work. I thought about opening a doggy daycare-type facility so dogs would have a safe place to hang out during the day. At the time there was no zoning for that kind of thing, so I didn't know how to set up such a service. Instead, I started offering poop scooping alongside my landscaping business, which allowed me to infiltrate dogs' homes, so to speak. For many of the pet owners I came to know through this job, it turned out that dog poop was the least of their worries.

Some of my clients were incredibly busy stay-at-home moms who didn't have time to train their dogs, given all their other responsibilities. One client was an elderly widow who humanized her dog, treating him like an infant, always carrying him around, petting him excessively, cooing at him with baby talk and lavishing toys and treats on him—while completely ignoring his basic doggy needs. That dog ran back and forth along the fence line of his backyard so much that a long strip of grass there had been worn down to dirt. I was clueless about what was going on in the majority of the other households because so many of my clients were out at work. Their dogs typically barked fanatically at me from behind their picture windows.

It was pretty obvious that there were a lot of depressed, bored, anxious, lonely, aggressive and unruly dogs out there in the world. I realized that I needed to get cracking on my dog daycare idea, and lucky for me, a dog came into my life at that point to steer me forward.

Dezdamona: Dog Guru

Dezdamona was a Border collie–Australian heeler cross. I always say that I didn't choose Dez; she chose me. My friend Colleen had her as a puppy, and whenever I visited her, Dez would treat me like some long-lost pal. She'd always jump into my VW Rabbit and sit there looking at me as if to say, "Okay, where are we going today?" She was always up for an adventure. When Colleen moved and wasn't allowed to have a dog in her new apartment, she called me. I went over to pick up five-month-old Dez, and she happily jumped into the car, raring to head off down the road with me. I remember her baying away as we drove along, putting on a show for the passing motorists, as if she was singing her heart out to her favourite song on the radio—an absolutely amazing dog.

Then somehow, one day, she escaped from the backyard. I went out and started combing the streets in panic. Eventually,

I found her in a field chasing butterflies—literally leaping into the air to play with them. And when she got tired of that, she took off again, and I followed her to a farmer's field, where she started herding a bunch of cows. "That dog's always here," said the farmer, "playing with my cattle."

No wonder Dez was such a contented dog. She'd given herself a whole rich life of her own. That's when I really appreciated how much exercise and stimulation a dog needs to have a good life. But we can't just let our dogs wander the streets all day, so how can we provide them with a mixed bag of activities—and safely?

Another important thing my dad taught me was that it's better to take risks in life than regret that you didn't. "The worst that can happen is that you'll make a mistake," he said. "And if you don't make mistakes, you're sure as heck not going to learn anything."

I decided to take the plunge and open up my first doggy daycare in my Calgary home. I started with just a handful of dogs. That posse and I spent most of our days running around the neighbourhood and going on field trips to various parks. By the end of the day, those pets were content to go home and sit around on their butts all night, chilling with their owners. Word spread that I was some sort of dog whisperer, but that wasn't the case. My clients' canines were simply getting exercise, mental stimulation and bonding time with other dogs. And I basically had a front-row seat to observe the ways dogs interact with each other.

It was really cool to learn these doggy rules of engagement and see how well even the most unruly animals adapted quickly to becoming part of a well-organized pack. Some of those dogs were clueless about canine socializing, which made them either shrinking violets or bullies. Either way, the well-socialized dogs treated them like weak links in a chain. They would isolate a rude and pushy dog from the rest of the pack, especially if the animal stepped out of line during playtime. Occasionally, they'd give the social misfit a quick peck or, in extreme cases, a nip. These dog disciplines never caused broken skin or any physical harm, but they certainly sent out a loud and clear message that any rogue behaviours in this pack were unacceptable.

The first time it happened, I tried to pull the just-scolded dog away, but she yelped and tugged at her leash as if to say, "Hey, I'm trying to have a conversation with my new buddy here. I'm trying to *learn* something." I dropped the leash, and she went right back to the dog who had disciplined her, but this time she didn't bare her teeth with insecurity or bark in his hairy ear. She was calm and collected, and they went about their bum-sniffing hellos without further incident.

But how to adapt those effective techniques to *human* training? One day, I was working with a client's dog—a nightmare Frankendog who flipped me the paw every time I tried to get him to sit and chill out. Dez was standing right behind me, watching as I struggled to figure out an effective way to get this dog to pay attention. She looked up at me as if to say, "Look, you don't know what you're doing. I'll show you." She came under my arm and, wham, she nailed the dog in the shoulder super-fast with her snout. He sat right down and looked at both of us. "Okay, I'm listening," he seemed to be saying. "What can you show me next?" It was brilliant. With a simple snap command, that dog was sitting consistently by the end of the day.

The key element of the move Dez made to get that dog's

respect and attention had nothing to do with brute force. It was all about lightning-fast speed. From the moment pups start moving around, their mothers are very strict in enforcing rules because they know that the consequences could be lethal. An eagle could swoop down to nab a straying pup or other carnivores could take matters into their own jaws. A dog disciplinary action might last only a second or two: a mother grabbing a pup by the scruff of the neck if she starts to stray too far from the litter or a dog whistling foul with an abrupt bark directed at the bully of the dog park. That's how Dez laid down the law. And watching her step in and act as surrogate teacher was an elegant lesson in dog leadership.

By comparison, people sometimes go on and on as they discipline their dogs, whether they get physical or they rant and rave at the dog verbally. But Dez taught me that when we humans adopt a disciplinary method that dogs understand and respect—one that relies on quick, decisive movement—we're speaking *their* language and we'll have much more success in getting them to listen to us.

So many of the dogs who stayed at my daycare operation went home to chaos and disharmony every night. And come Monday, after a whole weekend back with their owners, they'd be gong shows all over again. That's when I realized that a lot of human-dog relationships had nothing to do with the dogs' methods of communicating, socializing and living successfully together as a team. The more dogs and owners I met, the more I came to understand that many of the negative dog behaviours people wanted me to "fix"—excessive barking, yanking on the leash, bolting away at the park, ignoring commands, home wrecking and aggression—were actually natural canine responses to inappropriate *human* behaviours, attitudes and lifestyle choices. While many dog owners did the right thing by seeking out advice and guidance from dog trainers and vets, far too often that so-called professional guidance didn't include any methods that would help dogs learn to respect and cooperate with Two Legs outside a sterile training centre.

I realized that I needed to make the leap from part-time babysitter to trainer—and in order to do that effectively, I had to start training people; I had to get inside *their* heads.

I started dabbling in dog training with a client who was incredibly busy raising her two small kids. Her husband had heaped another responsibility on her by getting a dog, and she was resentful of that, but she knew she had to make the best of the situation by training her unruly pooch to respect her and obey her rules. I knew I'd have to adapt a dog-training program to her hectic schedule, so I recommended that she leash up her dog and connect for about two hours a day *while* she was doing all her daily chores: making breakfast, vacuuming, doing the laundry, talking on the phone, picking the kids up at school, preparing dinner—whenever she could fit it in. I suggested that while she was physically connected to the dog, she should incorporate basic sit-stay training into whatever she was doing, like while she was moving the laundry from the washer to the dryer, when she took the dog out to the car—whenever there was the opportunity to teach the dog to follow her commands.

I didn't know how the dog would respond, but when I came back the following week, he was paying close attention to her and obeying her commands, which naturally curbed the friction between them. Over the next few months, the busy mother persisted in wedging consistent daily training into her schedule of daily tasks and ended up having a stronger relationship with her dog than her husband had.

I thought I was onto something by mixing up training to suit an owner's busy, time-strapped life. That dog was literally following the mother's lead, and because she was always on the move, he was constantly stimulated, both physically and mentally. He was also getting a mixed bag of experiences that satisfied his needs and strengthened their bond.

At this point I knew I had to develop programs that custom-fit the needs of all sorts of different clients and their dogs. That's when another amazing dog entered my life to show me that by harnessing instead of resisting a dog's natural skills and talents, you're setting up a win-win situation of mutual respect.

To the Max with Maxamillion

Dez was nine years old when Max, an eight-month-old Border collie, entered our lives. Max's story was the same as Dez's: Natalie, a super friend of mine, couldn't keep Max in her new apartment. I can remember the day we picked him up at the airport as if it were yesterday. Peering out of the crate was a cute little floppy-eared pup.

Max was a happy-go-lucky dog, but he was also very curious about everything and like a tugboat when anything needed to be done. Max loved to work. He was always protecting clueless pups from aggressive dogs, and he was constantly drawn to kids and two-legged underdogs, wanting to be their bodyguard, keeping the bullies at bay. Max was the night guardian for my nieces and nephews, and I always tried to make a point of letting him do the work he wanted to do, so he'd feel useful and important.

Dez and Max were very different, but they had a tight bond that brought out the best in each other. Together, they really drove home the message that having a purpose in life is just as important for dogs as it is for humans. I think it's easy to lose sight of that with domestic dogs because we don't give them enough opportunities to apply their skills—herding, retrieving, protecting, even letting them lift our spirits by clowning around.

But trusting a dog to do what he or she wants to do while remaining safe and well behaved is kind of like trusting that your teenagers won't set your house on fire the first time you leave them home alone for the weekend. You know you have to leave them alone eventually, but it's hard for many people to take that leap. And how was I going to help other people build that bond of trust with their dogs when they could barely even control them on a simple walk around the block? I decided that the most practical way to maximize the training potential of both species was to throw a bunch of people and their dogs into a variety of real-life situations and get them moving around together.

I'll go into more detail about how I adapted my training methods to harness those unique dog skills very soon. But I must give credit where it's due. I honestly don't think I could have accomplished anything without Dez and Max as eager teaching assistants. As my helper dogs, they helped me train many people to understand the power and necessity of leadership by performing umbilical training (which I'll describe in Chapter 2) and helping dogs learn how to be dogs. Many of the dogs I'll talk about in this book were buddies of Max and Dez—including Rocky, Chopper, Bisco and Rudy the Schnoodle.

Max died four years ago, at the young age of twelve. He had a brutal disease called muscular myopathy, which causes degeneration of the muscle tissue. Because of the disease, one of his eyes had to be removed, and over the next few years, his health deteriorated to the point that he had a five-hour seizure. I decided I couldn't let my dog go through that again. It was so hard to see such a brave soul suffering. I knew I had to let him go.

I will never forget that terrible day. When we took him to the vet, Dez started to whimper and whine as soon as we pulled out of the driveway. Then she lay on top of Max in the back seat, sheltering and comforting him. She and I wept all the way to the cremation, and she was right there with me, putting Max's body into the incinerator. I physically buckled at the knees when we returned home and I saw Max's last meal untouched in his bowl. I lost a tremendous part of me when I lost Max, but over time I gradually gained bits of myself back, and eventually, I gained more strength than I'd ever had before. I am tearing up as I write this because he helped make me a better dog trainer and a better person.

Dez not only helped me get through that tough time but also helped me realize that a good dog is the best kind of teacher when it comes to living in the now. Naturally, Dez also took quite a while to mourn Max's passing, but one of the greatest blessings that dogs give us every single day is that they know how to move on. If you meet their dog needs, they can really teach you how to balance the past, present and future.

Dez died a year later, at the ripe old age of twenty-two. I keep Dez's and Max's ashes at my training centre in Kelowna, alongside the thirty-million-year-old dog skull. To this day, I see pieces of them in the dogs they helped me train. They were the driving force behind my determination to develop training methods that both dogs and people could actually wrap their heads and bodies around.

I also have to give a lot of credit to the many two-legged owners who are willing to put their dogs and themselves on the line to take this type of training. Many times we're fighting tooth and nail against years of bad training by so-called professionals. Typically, my clients will already have seen at least three trainers before I meet them, which just compounds the dog's confusion—like a kid who has three different history teachers in one year, all with their own ideas about the subject.

There are a few dog trainers out there who have put in the time and effort to study dogs and find training methods that actually set dogs and their owners up for success. I applaud and celebrate these people, along with the growing number of Certified Educator Trainers (CETs) who graduate from my school in Kelowna. I believe that, together, we can change the pathetically low training standards that currently characterize the industry. I also have faith that when dogs and humans are provided with education and skills in a motivating and stimulating environment—one that respects and fosters the pupils' intelligence, trusts in their abilities and allows room to explore their unique personalities—we'll be able to change the world, one trainer at a time, one family at a time.

What a Dog Wants, What a Dog Needs

Dogs have all sorts of great strengths and skills, but people often have the misconception that their seemingly boundless desire to use those abilities to please us is actually unconditional love. The truth is that with dogs, like humans, there are always strings attached. If you neglect them, dogs will make you pay—through a variety of negative behaviours, which I'll discuss in this book. I hope that once you understand why dogs do these perplexingly bad doggy things and once you've been given some sensible ways not only to fix them but also to help draw out your dog's unique personality, you'll have all the tools you'll need to enjoy a rich and wonderful bond with your four-legged buddy.

Let's go back to the similar needs of the thirty-million-year-old dog and the modern pooch. By harnessing these, whether in dog training exercises or in daily life, you'll have very effective methods for communicating with, teaching and bonding with your dog. Here's the list of prehistoric and present-day canine needs:

* The ability to function in an organized and healthy pack. For the majority of wild dogs and all domestic dogs that means being an obedient pack follower and learning the skills, rules and boundaries of that pack.
* Physical exercise and the freedom to safely explore the sights, sounds and smells of new environments.
* Socialization with other dogs.
* Mental stimulation that feeds the mind and gives the dog a sense of purpose in life.
* Play, bonding and affection.
* Lots of variety and the introduction of new training options through their entire lives to prevent the dog from becoming bored and stifled by routine.

These needs are pretty simple, right? Yet, too often, my clients misunderstand and misinterpret them, and they don't know how to successfully meet those needs in their own lives. In this book, I'll dig into some of the most common myths we have about dogs, dog training and interspecies bonding. But more importantly, I'll show you how to use your dog's needs, talents and ability to learn skills to help him become a cooperative and successful member of your team. Keep that thirty-million-year-old dog buddy in mind as you think about how alien and sometimes downright bizarre our modern world must appear to our dogs. Yet they try so hard to fit in, even when their behaviours seem to indicate the opposite.

We've opened up our lives and our homes to dogs for thousands of years. Isn't it about time we spent some time trying to open up our minds to understanding the dog's view? Dogs need a voice. I will be that voice while you learn *their* language.

The Key Factors for Successful Dog Training and Interspecies Bonding

Whether you're just getting started in training your new pup, looking to take your good relationship with your dog to a higher level or trying to correct negative dog behaviours, I'll provide step-by-step, do-it-yourself training material in each chapter, to help you teach your dog to be a well-adjusted member of your family. To get the ball rolling, take a look at this to-do list for successful training:

1. Have realistic expectations about your dog. Ditch the Lassie fantasies and other human baggage that unfairly burden your pet, and make sure the entire family unit participates in training and caring for her.

2. Establish clear and consistent leadership so your dog respects you as the pack leader and accepts his position as the pack follower. Once you're in the driver's seat, your dog will be primed and ready for training.

3. Learn to communicate in your dog's primary language: movement. Dogs can be taught to comprehend verbal cues and commands, but movements, gestures and actions that satisfy their basic needs are much more effective ways to teach them the skills they need to fit into a family pack.

4. Provide your dog with basic training that is adaptive to the rules of conduct in the canine world but that also allows her to function safely in the human world. This means giving her training exercises that feed her needs as well as her innate skills and intelligence. Don't use treats and other such ineffective props.

5. Give your dog a steady dose of physical exercise that allows him to roam the neighbourhood, explore new places and settings, socialize and play with other dogs. Let him earn the privilege of following his own nose, exploring the world off-leash, instead of being restricted to the distance your leash allows.

6. Establish and maintain consistent household rules and boundaries so your dog has a clear understanding of the rules of behaviour in the human world. Be a considerate and respectful human caregiver who appreciates how environmental changes—a new family member, a new job, a move, any two-legged conflicts—might negatively impact the dog.

7. Refrain from overcoddling your dog or forcing her into the role of surrogate human partner. Don't shower your dog with expensive and useless props and toys. Your dog should sleep in her own bed, have a maximum of three toys, a healthy four-legged diet and a few basic grooming aids to maintain physical

and mental health. Give your dog the gift of your time and reward your dog with games that satisfy her need for mental stimulation, play and affection. This approach will also stave off boredom, separation anxiety and negative behaviours and will allow your dog's skills and unique personality to shine through.

8. Don't consider adding a second dog to the family mix until your dog reaches a mature three years of age and has had a lot of socialization with other dog buddies. Some veterinarians tell people to get a second dog to reduce problem behaviours, but adding another dog to the mix often just adds fuel to the fire.

9. Start training your puppy from day one, and before you start shopping for a pup, become educated about the unscrupulous practices of some pet shops and breeders out there. Never take a pup home until it's at least eight, ideally nine, weeks of age, as this allows for critical bonding time with his mother and pup siblings.

10. Think about your relationship with your dog as a constantly evolving process. As dogs mature, they often go through phases that necessitate re-training—such as during the terrible twos and the golden years. Be considerate of these milestones and don't get stuck in strict routines that will bore your dog. Instead, find new ways to bond.

Autograph Hounds

My dog buddies and I get a lot of fan mail. These star dogs receive emails and love letters and are regularly stopped on the streets by adoring fans. Their fame doesn't swell their furry heads, though, and I think it's easy for me to stay grounded, thanks to them. People get stuck in ruts when they think they know best. When we box up our ideas and tie a neat bow around them, we are only fostering inflexibility and egomania. That's when the worst kinds of mistakes are made. That's when teachers become dangerous.

It's actually pretty easy being humble and motivated to do better work because I learn at least five things a day from dogs. I know that you can never have a dog completely figured out, so I'm always curious to learn more. Being around dogs 24/7 makes all of that easier, and even when I'm working with the most troubled families, it keeps me believing that the sun will shine through, even on the dark days. It'll take a lifetime to really understand dogs—I couldn't ask for a better way to spend mine.

CHAPTER ONE

Why Do You Want a Dog?

SETTING REALISTIC EXPECTATIONS FOR A WIN-WIN RELATIONSHIP

MYTH: Any dog can easily fit into your family unit at any point in your life.

REALITY CHECK: You should carefully consider *why* you want a dog in your life, what kind of dog you want and what a successful interspecies relationship means to you before you even think about shopping for a dog. Having a dog will likely be at least a sixteen-year commitment, but it can become a prison sentence for both species—and the dog too often pays the ultimate price, with his or her life.

The Doggy Dogma Assessment

When I first meet a client, I ask them three really important questions. It's not a pop quiz that I can mark with a pass or fail grade in red ink. That would mean I believe I know the one right answer to each question, but I don't. Although some people love "playing God" in this way, I don't feel I have the right to do that.

The first question is "Why do you want a dog?" Or if my client already owns a dog, "Why *did* you want a dog?" The second question is "What do you want your dog to be able to do?" And last but not least, I ask, "What does success mean to you in a dog-human relationship?" I pose these questions because my clients' responses give me some fascinating insights into their frame of mind, as well as a family's dynamics and their expectations not only about the role they want that dog to play in their life but also about how they imagine *their own* life.

Until recently, the answer to these three questions was probably much simpler in most cases: "I want a dog to herd cattle"; " . . . to protect the flock of sheep from predators"; " . . . to help with the hunting." Nobody is sure exactly why humans decided to roll out the red carpet for dogs, but one theory is that the least skittish and aggressive wild canines were the most likely to be curious about us and the most willing to interact with us. In fact, anthropologists have theorized that when we started living with dogs fifteen thousand years ago—a time when it is believed domestic dogs diverged from their wolf ancestors[1]—we mostly cherry-picked the ones that were naturally submissive and friendly, so they've evolved to get along with us.[2] That makes sense to me. You wouldn't be able to develop a bond with a dog that bolted as soon as it saw, heard or smelled you coming.

Anthropologists and archaeologists have dug up a lot of evidence to support their theories that dogs have had an intimate relationship with humans for a long time. The oldest dog burial site found to date is about fourteen thousand years old. It's in Germany, about an hour south of Düsseldorf, and the dog skeleton there looks like that of a small sheepdog. But the buried remains of dogs have been found all over the world, often alongside those of humans.[3]

So if you have a dog, you are part of an ancient tradition—though you likely had different motivations for owning a canine than the humans who hunted or travelled with dogs so many centuries ago. In this chapter, I'll talk about the many reasons people choose to have dogs in their lives and their various expectations about the kind of relationship they want with them. As I mentioned earlier, it's great to have expectations about our dogs and it's important to set goals for both species. But some expectations simply don't fit in with our own lifestyles. So many people saddle both themselves and their dogs with unrealistic, and sometimes downright impossible, hopes and dreams. And those expectations often underestimate or utterly ignore the skills and needs of dogs.

WE'RE IN THIS TOGETHER

Dogs have been helping humans for a long time. In some regions, herding, hunting and sled dogs still work by our sides, helping us survive. Nowadays, we also have guide dogs, rescue dogs, police dogs, de-mining dogs (dogs who detect land mines) and dogs that detect cancer.[4] Dog companions can have a therapeutic effect on people who have anything from heart disease to mental illnesses. Recent dog DNA sequencing has also revealed that they have much the same DNA as humans,[5] so gene research with dogs is helping crack a variety of human diseases.[6]

In the past decade or two, dogs have also become a hot topic among behavioural scientists at universities all over the globe.[7] Chimps might be our species' closest relatives, but researchers have recently found that dogs are better than chimps at problem solving and at perceiving and responding to human methods of communication, such as pointing, nodding, glancing and other specific body and facial cues.[8] Dogs have also been found to be better than their closest relative, the wolf, at problem solving because they've evolved with humans for at least fifteen thousand years. Even six-week-old puppies still living with their four-legged moms respond to humans, which suggests that they are evolutionarily predisposed to follow our cues.[9]

You Complete Me, Rover

A common response to the "Why do you want a dog?" question is "I had a dog as a kid." That answer sounds pretty simple, but there are usually some really interesting back-stories involved when a client says something like that. If you've thought the same, maybe you have beautiful, gold-tinged memories of running through the woods with Rover. You might want to recapture your youth and a simpler "dog days of summer" time in your life when you didn't have a care in the world. Or you might want a second crack at that "dog that got away"—whether she ran away from home, never to be found again, or your parents sent her off to "a better place," which you now know was actually the animal shelter.

Another common response that clients give, and you

might, too, is that they always wanted a dog but their parents wouldn't allow it. If you've thought along those lines, you might have spent half your life feeling ripped off, and having a dog might be a sort of rite of passage into adulthood.

Some people I encounter are planning to have kids in a few years, and they think of the dog as a sort of practice child. Others want a replacement for a dog that recently died. Some are looking for protection. I know a single woman whose home was invaded by five guys. They raped her and killed her German shepherd. She now has two huge dogs; she *needs* them to feel safe. Others have had a failed relationship or even a string of them, and they're sick and tired of the two-legged letdowns. So they bring a dog into their world to ease the pain and loneliness, to keep them company and, in some cases, to stand in as a surrogate partner or friend that they can take mountain biking or cuddle with on the couch.

Balancing a hectic life is another reason people get a dog. Rocky's "parents," Steve and Peggy, are hard-working professionals: self-described DINKs (Double Income, No Kids). Before Rocky entered their lives, they'd typically cap their long workdays with late dinners in a restaurant. Neither Peggy nor Steve had any previous experience with dogs, but they thought it would help balance their hectic schedules and, in Peggy's words, "force us to have a home life." As you'll find out later, their real-life experience with Rocky was nothing like this initial picture of domestic bliss.

Other people get a dog because they're depressed or have a physiological illness and their doctor suggests that a dog companion would help balance their health. Sure, studies have found that dogs are great stress busters; they can help us stay physically active and provide us with healthy social companionship.[10] Being with dogs can elevate mood and lower blood pressure and stress.[11] But we need to be able to provide our dogs with a lot of physical and mental activities so they can also be as healthy and happy as possible. We should be stable on our own two legs and know where we're going to be for the next decade before committing to owning a dog. A dog sure can inject sunshine into your life, but he can't do that alone. He's not a magic genie who can grant all your wishes, especially if you expect him to be the spitting image of your favourite childhood dog or that incredible dog who passed away. If you think your dog will automatically set you up for a better life, whatever that means to you, you—and your dog—will be miserable. There's a lot of hard work involved, so you'd better be ready to make the effort.

CANINE-HUMAN CO-EVOLUTION

Pioneering dog researchers at the Family Dog Project in Budapest, Hungary, summed up the strong dog-human connection by saying that "there is a large overlap" between the ways humans and dogs behave "because during their evolution in close contact with human groups, dogs evolved functionally similar social skills." Studying these similar behaviours "widens our possibility for understanding human social cognition."[12]

In other words, dogs aren't slobbering idiots. Complex things are actually going on under their furry hoods. And understanding dog behaviours allows us to better understand human behaviours.

Lassie Come Home

Other people have what I call "Hollywood syndrome": whether they're five years old or fifty, they have a bunch of sentimental dog movies looping through their heads. They think that having the golden retriever, the Dalmatian(s) or the Lassie dog will automatically open up some magical, perfect world, complete with the dancing, the music and the Technicolor. People get so caught up in the fantasy that they can't see the amazing dog-in-waiting sitting right in front of them.

Movie-star dogs have to go through months and even years of training and education. Like human movie stars, they're surrounded by a team of professionals: a number of different trainers, stylists and makeup artists, sitters, managers, agents, lawyers, as well as canine stunt doubles and stand-in dogs to do certain scripted tricks. How can a typical family compete with these pro dogs? They can't, and they shouldn't even think of trying. But some dog owners refuse to let go of their illusions and choose to believe that somehow they got a doggy dud and there's a better Lassie out there somewhere. Too often, that means the entire family unit has to suffer through a sixteen-year prison sentence or the dog gets packed off to the animal shelter or put to death. Whatever happens, it's certainly not a pretty picture after all.

Before you start shopping around for a dog, ask yourself why you want one, and do your best to make sure that you're starting your relationship with realistic expectations. If it's too late for that, it's still a perfect time to start training yourself to be aware of your own expectations of your dog and of yourself.

Custom-Designed Canines

When I ask my second question, "What do you want your dog to be able to do?", people often respond by telling me that they want a certain breed. In my opinion, our culture is much too breed-centric about dogs. Instead of really digging into what kind of relationship they want with their dogs, people often focus on the look of the dog.

While it's important to choose a breed that fits your lifestyle and your needs, remember that every dog has a unique personality. People will say, "Well I had a Labrador seven years ago who was so calm and mellow" and assume that's how all Labs will be. They don't realize they're describing a dog's *personality*. They get another Lab and feel let down because she isn't like that at all.

Imagine if you expected that from children: "Oh, the first baby was so sweet and mellow, she slept through the night and rarely ever cried. But the new one . . . We can't get a night's sleep anymore! We can't figure out why he's not an exact match!" You wouldn't think that about people, so why view dogs in that way? Every member of your family should be on the same page, or at least in the same book, when they commit first to getting a dog and second to defining what kind of dog suits their lives. But family members will often have very different wants and expectations that would be impossible for any dog to live up to. To illustrate the point, here's a dialogue I recently had with a married couple:

WIFE: I want a pug.

BRAD: Okay, that's a shorthaired breed. It will need to wear a coat in winter if you want to spend a lot of time outdoors.

HUSBAND: I want a bulldog.

WIFE: What about a husky?

BRAD: How'd you go from pug to husky!?

WIFE: They're beautiful and fluffy.

HUSBAND: I don't want a dog that needs grooming. I want a dog I can take for runs on the beach.

BRAD: Sounds romantic. Why don't you take your *wife* to the beach?

HUSBAND: She's not a runner.

BRAD: And you wouldn't put your wife on a leash and expect her to chase after you for seven kilometres, yanking at her to keep moving when she gets tired or wants to pause to talk to a friend, right?

HUSBAND: Of course not!

BRAD: Then why expect that from a dog? Even dogs that like to run long distances need to stop periodically to smell the territory and check out old and new dog buddies along the way. You need to be willing to do that.

WIFE: I just want something to cuddle with.

BRAD: Sweet. Why don't you cuddle with Two Legs? He's there 24/7 for you.

WIFE AND HUSBAND (in unison): Oh, Brad, don't be crazy!

What's so crazy about assuming that a married couple should meet each other's needs for companionship, love and affection instead of expecting a dog to fill that role? There's nothing crazy about having *realistic* expectations of our dogs, like wanting to have a dog that can go off-leash, is well-behaved around kids, respects our human possessions and doesn't have a meltdown every time we set foot out of the house. Canines don't come to us pre-programmed like computers, so it's our job to teach them how to do these things. And if we're not meeting their needs, they will rebel. No dog could possibly live up to a wild mix of *human* expectations and be a healthy, well-adjusted *dog*. They don't come with an on-off switch that can be used to shut down inappropriate human expectations. And they don't come with a two-year warranty, though like appliances, they often fall apart around that time, and far too often, it's only then that owners go looking for someone to "fix" the dog.

There's no shortage of doggy mechanics out there who are willing to peek under the hood, diagnose the dog's issues in a seemingly authoritative voice and promise to quick-fix anyone's troubled pet. Some will even provide a warranty or claim to provide you with lifelong training. Even if they live up to that promise, why would you give them a second chance to wreck your dog even more? Too many dog trainers will actually screw your dog up on the first go, kind of like the shady car mechanic who messes with your brakes, carburetor and windshield wipers along the way, even though these parts had no problems *before* you walked into the shop. I'll get into the dog trainer con artists in greater detail in Chapter 4, but for now let's just say the pet industry is a dog-eat-dog world. I've seen many dogs with great potential turned into ticking time bombs because of bad training.

Dogs, Not Bombs

Too often, it's my job to defuse that ticking time bomb or pick up the pieces after the explosion. I love working with dogs, but I don't exactly relish being called in as a "last resort." I'd much rather start educating dog owners *before* they've begun window shopping at pet stores or cruising dog shelters, and certainly before they bring a four-legged friend into their lives.

Considering the bizzaro state of current interspecies relations, I guess you could call my picture a sort of fantasy too. But I don't expect perfection in myself or my dogs and ditto for my clients and their dogs. Flaws, quirks, frailties, self-esteem issues and biases are just parts of any relationship package, and in my mind, there's no such thing as an off-the-rack training program. With dog training, one size *does not* fit all.

All animals foster their young and teach them how to survive and prosper in a happy, contented life. If we choose to bring a dog into our lives, it's our job to take over those reigns and do our best to protect and safeguard our dogs. But if they're going to fit into our pack, they need our leadership first and foremost. Failure to establish and maintain consistent leadership with dogs is the number one reason interspecies relationships start going off track. And dogs can get even more messed up when they're forced to play wishbone to caregivers with incompatible ideals about how to raise the dog. A dog can't possibly function healthfully around that kind of human friction. I've seen firsthand how problem dog behaviours escalate in that kind of environment, and sometimes those issues become the tipping point in a relationship, leading to divorce and ugly custody battles. Sometimes I think I've seen it all, but then a new client pitches me another goopy curve ball or someone emails my website with crime scene photos of a good dog gone bad, and I realize there are still more problems out there than I imagined.

Deadly Consequences of Human Neglect

Millions of dogs are abandoned, sent to shelters and euthanized every year. How many of these dogs could have been saved if their needs had been met and they'd been offered some sensible, practical training? More than we would like to know. But I create some of these statistics myself because I am sometimes obliged to make the call to euthanize a dog. It's the worst part of my job. Nine times out of ten, dogs who end up being put to death because of apparently incorrigible behaviours sent out warning signs for many years that were lost in translation or ignored by their human caregivers.

Bad behaviours sometimes include biting, and every year, there are about 4.5 million of those in the United States alone.[13] In far too many cases, the biting dogs became aggressive because they were neglected by a string of individuals long before they lashed out: bad breeders, pet store operators who hawked puppies who'd been ripped from their litters weeks before they should have been and owners who failed to make sure that their dog's needs were met. Aside from the rare dog with neurological damage, dogs aren't born killers. They don't wake up thinking, "Hmm, can't wait to bite the hand that feeds me." But that's exactly what happens when their needs are not met. After all, they're carnivores with forty-two teeth, just like wolves and foxes and they can use them to injure or kill when they've been mistreated or neglected.

We've all read the occasional news stories about killer dogs (and subsequent breed bans in some American states) that vilify certain dogs, when in reality, these animals are the victims of bad breeders, trainers and owners. Dog breed profiling fails to take into account all the recent academic research that has found little to no correlation between specific breeds and behaviours but instead underlines the personalities of individual *dog owners* in shaping dogs' characteristics.[14] Whatever the dog breed, we ignore that important factor at the peril of both species.

TRAINING SAVES DOGS' LIVES

*S*ixty-three per cent of American households have a dog, but millions are abandoned and sent to shelters every year.[15] Only 16 per cent of these shelter dogs are adopted, and approximately five million dogs and cats are euthanized annually. Statistics from the National Council on Pet Population revealed that a whopping 96 per cent of dogs shipped to shelters had received absolutely no training.[16]

Pet Detective

The third question I ask my clients is probably the toughest of all because it often gets to the deeper issues in people's lives. Asking someone to define what a successful dog-human relationship is in their view sometimes means putting all their cards on the table about their own life and looking at whether they're meeting their own goals and definitions of success. If you were asked this question, you might say that when you first got your dog, success meant being able to go on off-leash hikes every weekend. But maybe the demands of your job got in the way; you're now often working weekends and there's barely time for quick walks around the block. Your life is stressful and your dog isn't getting what he needs, so even those short walks become tug-o'-war matches.

When dog relations come under strain, those hopes and expectations go out the window and people revert to a sort of survival mode. Many of my clients become prisoners in their own homes because they're too afraid to step outside with the dog. That kind of siege mentality just makes matters worse for everyone.

Of course, these problems don't develop overnight. Many of my dog clients' negative behaviours have been going on for years, but they haven't taken them seriously enough until the dog does something really bad or there's an impending change: a baby is on the way, a new partner is laying down the "It's Me or Rover" ultimatum or the dog bit another dog, for example. So now, not only do they have to fix learned behaviours and bad habits; they have to do it within a short period of time—or else!

But you can't fix a dog if there are issues among the human pack members. I'm no marriage counsellor or family therapist, but I often have to find creative ways to get people operating in harmony before they can start doing the same with their dogs—like asking a couple to take dance lessons while their teen kids work on dog training or incorporating some dog training into a family picnic to build up a family's teamwork skills. The goal is to get people bonding and communicating with each other effectively. That often means getting honest and acknowledging that they've veered away from their own hopes and ideals about a successful family life.

With dog training, every single member of the family unit should be 100 per cent on board, acting as a team to provide coordinated and consistent structure. People sometimes need to be reminded that *any* good relationship doesn't just fall into their laps tied up with a pretty bow— it takes time and effort, openness to change and some sacrifices along the way.

———

The Pre-Pet Questionnaire

I totally appreciate those people who go for pre-pet coun-selling long before they start window shopping for a new dog. Some of you will roll your eyes at that idea, thinking it sounds like a hokey, new-fangled therapy. But it's the ideal way to start on the path to success. I also recommend that you think about the following factors before you decide to bring a dog into your life:

* Your life plans in two years (when dogs reach social maturity), five years (when dogs typically hit mid-life and might need some re-training, along with new forms of stimulation) and ten years (when dogs become seniors). If your own life goals include a lot of travel or an intensive work schedule, you might not have enough time to adequately train and bond with your dog during these critical periods.

* Whether you plan to have children in the next few years. If so, it's ideal to get a dog at least two years before you introduce a child to the household.

* Whether your children are currently old enough to participate in training and bonding with your dog. It's best to wait until your youngest child is at least three years of age.

* If you're currently single, whether you plan to start a serious relationship within the next few years. Your future partner might fall for you but not necessarily your dog—and your dog might not like your partner much either.

* If you're already in a committed relationship, whether both of you can dedicate the time and energy to caring for and bonding with a dog. If you're going

through a rocky patch, consider holding off getting a dog until your relationship is back on track.

Recap: Why Do You Want a Dog?

Whether you're thinking about adding a dog to your life or you already have one in your family pack, I hope you'll take some time to think about why you want a dog, what kind of relationship you want with that dog and how you define success in the mix, so you have a realistic set of goals before you start training your pet to become a healthy member of your family pack.

If you already have a dog and this process makes you realize you had unrealistic expectations or weren't well prepared to devote the necessary time and effort needed to train and bond with that dog, don't beat yourself over the head about the what-ifs related to your past—my intentions are quite the opposite! Just acknowledge those factors so you can move forward with a new set of goals.

Before we get into the hands-on training, here's a quick recap of some important factors to consider before you bring a dog into your family, or at least before you start a new training program with your canine companion:

* Interview yourself and every member of your family pack about why you want a dog in the family, how you want to share your life with that dog and what a successful interspecies bond means to you.
* Identify the myths, fantasies and unrealistic expectations that might negatively impact your relationship with your dog—and do your best to avoid saddling your dog with fairy-tale ideals.

* Choose a breed that best fits your lifestyle, but remember that each dog has her own unique personality and that, just like humans, no two dogs are identical.
* Make sure that all members of the family unit are willing to help care for your dog, provide consistent leadership and spend time meeting the dog's basic needs for exercise, mental stimulation, play and a mixed bag of different activities that nourish his need to be an active, useful, engaged member of your family.
* Don't expect perfection from your dog or from yourself. Dog training can be time consuming and challenging, so never expect a quick-fix, especially if your pet has developed problem behaviours. If you decide to work with a trainer, be wary of those who promise fast-track training. You might just be setting yourself up as a repeat customer—or, worse, that training might damage your dog even more.
* Never forget that while a dog has many needs that are similar to ours, they are also related to wild dogs and wolves. Don't live in fear of your dog's canine instincts, but be watchful and respectful of how those instincts can have deadly consequences.
* The best way to prime your dog for success is to define your own personal life goals first and to assess whether you've strayed away from them. Develop and fortify your bonds with everyone in the family so that you're in sync with each other when you start dog training.
* If you're thinking about getting a dog, consider going for pre-pet counselling or sit down and assess your life

plans for at least the next decade. If you don't have a basic road map plotted for yourself, consider holding off on dog ownership until you do.

CHAPTER TWO

Leader of the Pack

ASSERTING YOUR ALPHA STATUS

MYTH: A dog who always assumes the lead role is simply a confident, playful and energetic dog.

REALITY CHECK: Handing your dog the role of dominant member of the pack is the number one cause of the many problem dog behaviours described in this book. Forcing your dog to lead the human family puts far too much stress on the dog and wreaks havoc on everyone.

De-Throning King Chopper

Chopper was the neighbourhood bully when I met him. The two-year-old golden retriever had bitten a total of four dogs, sticking his owners Dan and Heather with hundreds of dollars in vet bills and a bad rep. "On walks, that seventy-five-pound dog was impossible to control," says Dan. "He dragged us around everywhere and would run rampant. He never listened to us—especially Heather. It was a mess." Things got even messier when the couple had their first child. "He never showed aggression with people, but after the baby arrived, he became extra-protective as soon as we set foot outside."

"We didn't think about it at the time, but Chopper was definitely the household alpha," says Dan. "He slept in our bed and sat on the couch, and he was always bolting to the door and jumping up on visitors when they walked through the door. We knew that if we didn't get Chopper in line quick, we'd have to get rid of him."

In short, Chopper needed alpha training exercises—and in this chapter, I'll walk you through those exercises. They anchor all my methods for teaching your dog to be a brilliant family pack member and a great dog citizen. In almost every situation I'm called into, the basic reason for the chaos is that the dog is running the household. With Chopper, as with every alpha dog, the priority was to de-throne him and teach him to respect his owners as the household CEOs. My methods for doing this harness a dog's natural desire to be a content, well-balanced pack member, but just as importantly, they train *humans* to develop and maintain pack leadership.

When it comes to human pack status, there are hundreds of colours in the crayon box. Our various roles in the world are too complex and nuanced to be defined as either dominant or submissive; the hues, shades and lines are always blurred. But for human-domestic dog relations, there are no shades—only black and white, yellow or red. Whenever we take the submissive role with our dogs, we're introducing a different colour to the mix that confuses her and leaves her no choice but to assume the alpha role. When that happens, the dog will be much more resistant to learning basic skills and following commands. All sorts of behavioural issues will arise as a result, including excessive barking, home wrecking, separation anxiety, insecurities and even highly aggressive behaviours. The main problem is that the dog thinks she's in charge. And the more you try to correct those issues with quick-fixes like treat training and other nonsense, the more power that dog will have over everyone. When people neglect their responsibility to be the dog's leader, the dog scores a win and will continue to act out to score more wins, even if the behaviours are negative. Telling your dog that you don't like that behaviour isn't getting through to the dog as a negative because she's always in control—and she's getting a lot of attention from it. Usually, the attention—your reaction to the bad behaviour—is highly emotionally charged, which the dog picks up on as a loud and clear signal that you are weak, distressed or even in pain. That means she has to up the power ante again. Maybe she'll bark more furiously the next time you leave the house or let it rip on the new couch. This generates more anxiety for both species and leaves everyone chasing their tails round and round and round.

One of the coolest things about dogs is that if you give them a very clear lesson, they adapt to your human position of authority very easily, just as they accept the guidance of their mothers during their first weeks of life. But if you keep switching back and forth between playing lead and follower, changing up the dynamics with inconsistencies, the dog will never understand her place in the family. She'll try really hard to understand, but I've seen dogs stare at the owner and then literally scratch their heads and look at them as if to say, "You know what? You have nothing to offer me, so I'm just gonna go sniff around over there." The dog has given up trying to understand what Two Legs is on about. People have to rec-ognize that *they're* dropping the ball, not the dog.

Dogs are extremely observant of sensory details, *all the time*. They're always picking up on even the subtlest cues to assess their place in the pack. So every time you let that dog lead, whether he's the first to step out the front door or he thinks he's free to bark like crazy whenever someone passes by, it's a strong signal to the dog that he is in charge.

We humans wear a lot of different hats—parent, child, partner, boss, client, employee and sometimes all in one day—but dogs have only two choices. (And please don't stick a hat on your dog!) If her human pack members aren't taking the lead, she'll feel obliged to take the reigns.

Imagine how stressful that must be. It'd be like telling the three-year-old to pick up the siblings from soccer, cook dinner, do the laundry and pay the bills—in another lan-guage! By not asserting calm, clear, consistent and trust-worthy authority over your dog, you're just setting her up for failure. In order for dogs to feel safe, protected and content in a world *we* created and brought them in to, they need to know that every single Two Legs in the family is their boss.

Pack Leaders: The Good, the Bad and the Ugly

There are a lot of misconceptions floating around about the term "alpha." Some might say that it means being a bully, a tyrant or physically abusive in order to assert pack leadership. People think of it in old-school military boot camp terms, and unfortunately, there are still some trainers out there who beat dogs into submission. On the flip side, there's another so-called "positive reinforcement" trend whereby owners are urged to use *treats* to lure dogs into submission. In reality, treats do anything but that.

Some people also bring in their own negative human baggage. One of my clients had a tough time asserting alpha status with her dog because every time she tried to discipline bad behaviour, she thought about the hell she'd suffered as a kid with an abusive mother. Child abuse boils my blood, but this client's reaction is another example of how we overhumanize our dogs and project our own experiences onto them. I'm certainly not saying that it's okay to be physically abusive of dogs, but I've studied wild dogs, coyotes and wolves, and I know their packs are highly organized and highly disciplined—they have to be in order to survive. In the wild, the pack leader will discipline other pack members swiftly if they get out of line, typically with a peck or nip, but in many cases with very aggressive actions. As long as the pack is strong, dogs know that fighting with the leader is a bad idea, just like we know that clocking the human boss isn't an acceptable or advantageous approach in the workplace. Every member of the dog pack knows there's strength in numbers and that power struggles rock the boat, potentially leading to serious physical harm. The beaten dog will be left behind to perish, and the pack will be minus a team player.

With wild dogs, pack members are more than content to be followers while still acting as part of an efficient team. As long as the pack leader is respectful and trustworthy, directing them to food and away from danger, they've got no worries. Subordinate dogs don't grudgingly tag behind, sulking, whining and plotting to overthrow the leader. We wouldn't think about putting kids in the driver's seat to run the family show, so why put a dog in charge?

With human–dog packs, we need to establish and consistently maintain rules of behaviour that foster the health and safety of dogs and everyone they meet. It's up to us to teach them the rules, and we can't do that unless they trust and respect us to take the lead. Being alpha means setting clearly defined boundaries for the dog so she understands and appreciates those rules. It also means interrupting negative behaviours as they are starting—like jumping up on human friends, lunging for the open front door, stealing food and peeing on the carpet—to prevent those things from actually happening. And if the bad deed has already been done, clear disciplinary action must be taken so that your pooch knows those behaviours are unacceptable.

People will argue that you shouldn't always be disciplining a dog. Right! I totally agree. If you provide concise and clear training, you won't need to discipline your dog all the time. Just the same, even when you've established your alpha position, don't expect every negative dog behaviour to vanish into thin air, especially for dogs who have been playing household CEO for years. As I'll describe in Chapter 10, new or recurring bad behaviours may also crop up periodically as your dog matures. But you'll be able to curb them if your dog always respects that you're the boss. I assure you that if you maintain alpha status and provide your dog with the basic training presented in the following chapters, your dog will be happy to take a load off and relax while you run the show.

Respect Is a Two-Way Street

I'm going to talk about the principle methods for alpha training in a minute. But first I want to clarify that while it's of the utmost importance to take the lead role in your dog's life from the get-go, it's also imperative that you satisfy all of his basic doggy needs. If your dog is underexercised, understimulated or overcoddled, he will rebel against you, no matter how much alpha training you do.

After all, if you're not respecting your dog's needs, why should your dog respect yours? Dogs should be willing to work to prove their worthiness to you, but you also need to do the same. Nobody should expect perfection, and we need to keep the dog's unique personality in mind, just as we need to respect a human's characteristics. You can't change every quirk and you shouldn't want to. The ultimate goal is to let that dog's brilliant self shine through, whether she's a mellow couch potato, a gregarious social butterfly or a rambunctious busybody.

Alpha Think

We've all met those badly behaved kids who have tantrums whenever they don't get what they want. Some kids treat their parents like servants and ATM machines all rolled into one. When it comes to discipline, rules and boundaries, it's as if the parents are afraid of their own kids, so they let the kids set the rules instead. Of course, that's a recipe for disaster, and when I explain it this way to most dog owners, they get it immediately.

The same rules apply to obnoxious alpha dogs. They need to know and respect that their owners are the bosses. And to earn that respect, the adults need to lay down rules, boundaries and a clear understanding of accountability. Otherwise, alpha dogs will never be able to trade in their crowns for a peaceful, balanced life.

Alpha training is the critical first step during the first two weeks of training any dog, whether you're teaching your young pup how to get along, working to enhance your relationship with your mature dog or dealing with a delinquent home wrecker or a pet who has separation anxiety. Providing pack leadership is essential to all the basic training methods I'll be discussing in the next three chapters—and all of these exercises should be incorporated into the first two weeks of training. Together, they set the tone for establishing and maintaining a stellar bond with your dog, so you can truly get to know her and take your relationship to higher levels—like giving your dog the freedom to go off-leash, which I'll tell you how to do in Chapter 5.

Alpha Dog Test

Not sure if your dog thinks he's running the family circus? Here are some telltale signs that your pooch has assumed the role of pack leader.

* He's always pulling at the leash, taking the lead position on walks and trying to control his movements—and yours!
* He's always jumping up on other dogs and people or growling and barking excessively to take on a dominant and protective role.
* She hogs the human furniture, particularly the bed and the couch, and growls territorially when she's expected to share these spaces.
* She ignores you when you use basic commands like "Sit," "Stay" and "Come."
* She cooperates with your commands when it suits her, but when it doesn't, she tries to manipulate you, either by growling aggressively or by showing exaggerated submissiveness—such as shrieking as if she's in pain,

twirling around in circles or dropping down and
rolling over like a diva who's had her crown stolen.

Watch out for any of these signs of master manipulation. They
are indications that your dog is challenging your leadership.
These manipulative tactics then become learned behaviour
when owners have a track record of submitting and caving
in to their dog's controlling behaviours.

Alpha What-You-Need Checklist

These are the three key things you'll need to begin alpha
training:

* ★ a good leash
* ★ a good collar
* ★ a big bag of focus, consistency and patience, especially
  if your dog has been playing alpha for many years

Leashes and collars are the most important tools for dog
training. In fact, they're the only two you'll need for alpha
training. They literally establish a connection between you
and your dog, so it's imperative that you make this bond as
safe, comfortable and stress-free as possible by investing in a
good leash and a good collar.

I advise owners to use a six-foot (about two-metre) lead
because shorter leashes will stifle your dog, increasing anxiety
and resentment—and this is not a good way to set the tone for
getting in sync with your dog and bonding with him. Longer
leashes and extending leashes are too dangerous and completely
useless in terms of maintaining control over your dog. Harness
rigs are also useless because they're designed for sled dogs.
They'll force your dog to pull, which automatically puts them

in the driver's seat. Use a strong nylon leash that's about three-quarters of an inch wide (about two centimetres wide).

When it comes to collars, you need to find something that's humane but that will also allow you to react quickly to bad behaviours and act as an extended hand for correction purposes. I'm totally against choke chains and pinch collars because they cause pain during the entire walk and can damage your dog both physically and emotionally—I think they should be banned! I recommend a Martingale collar, which was created for horse training and adapted for dogs. It consists of a fabric section and a short chain rigged with a metal ring that attaches to the leash. The design allows the collar to be secure but also comfortable unless the leash is strained, in which case, the part of the chain that connects to the fabric collar tightens and the part connected to the leash extends. (Picture the chain as a circle that triangulates when there's friction on the leash.) This allows your dog freedom to move around while you maintain control. The Martingale

collar also lets you use quick movements to correct your dog when she pulls on the leash, but it will loosen immediately, so there's no danger of inflicting pain or potentially harming the dog either physically or emotionally. Look for the Martingale-style "Hustle Up" collar that I designed (it's available at pet stores and online at www.bradpattison.com). Make sure, too, that the collar you buy has metal loops and buckle clasps. They're better than plastic ones because plastic will break over time. Check the collar and leash periodically to make sure the loops are still tight, especially if you have a big dog. Before you put the Martingale collar onto your dog, test it on your hand first. You'll notice that a quick pull on the leash will cause you absolutely no pain or discomfort.

Focus, patience and consistency are also key with alpha training—as with any dog training. If you're frazzled and tired and can't focus on the task at hand, your mind will wander or you'll become frustrated and stressed out during the process. Your dog will naturally pick up on those emotions and he'll either see them as weaknesses and take the reigns or he'll become frustrated and confused. You need to approach alpha training with energy and determination so your dog understands that you're in control. You can't pull that off if you're so stressed that you throw hissy fits and vent your frustrations on your dog.

Umbilical Training: The Alpha Lifeline

I call my type of alpha training "alpha umbilical training." It's so simple, but it's the absolutely key method for establishing your alpha position. I use the word "umbilical" because during training, your dog will be on a leash attached to your waist. And when you've finished the training, your dog will be so tuned into you and primed to follow your directions that it will be as if you're joined to each other by an umbilical cord. Alpha umbilical training should happen during the first two weeks, and it should be combined with my no talking rule, which strengthens your ability to bond in your dog's primary language: movement. I'll describe the no talking rule and other canine communication principles in Chapter 3, so be sure to read that chapter before you start your alpha umbilical training.

To begin an umbilical session, put the dog's leash around your waist and thread the collar clip through the leash handle so you have something that looks like a belt. Leash the dog up to the Martingale collar and start walking around as if she wasn't even there. The goal is to dictate every movement, which gets your dog paying attention to you and following your lead.

* Wherever you go, make sure you're always in the lead: going through doorways (especially the front and back outside doors of your house and other buildings), walking up and down the stairs, hustling to answer the

phone and taking your daily walks.

* Whenever your dog gets even a step in front of you or tries to block your movement, change your direction so you're always in the lead.
* Don't touch the leash; pretend it's not even there.
* If your dog gets in your path at any point, don't move *around* your dog; make your dog learn to respect your movements and get out of your way. That doesn't mean that you should treat your dog like a soccer ball and kick her in the side or hammer down on her paws. Even if you put very light, gentle pressure on her paw, she will probably move out of the way.
* The key here is that you control the movements so your dog learns to move with you. Your dog is not a piece of furniture, and she will quickly learn that she needs to be alert to your movements and get out of your way.
* At first, your striding legs might make physical contact with your dog's body, or if you have a big dog, you might have to assert leg pressure against her side, but don't be hesitant about continuing to move forward.
* If your dog keeps standing in your way and you find that you're stepping around her, find a sidewalk or large space where you can keep yourself on a straight path for at least twenty feet (about six metres).
* Every time she gets in the way, continue to move in a straight line.
* If you make even the slightest sideways step to avoid contact with your dog during this process, go back to the beginning of the sidewalk and start walking again until she learns to walk by your side and steer clear of *you*.

* Sometimes you may need to do a leash correction (which I'll describe a bit later in this chapter).
* Each time you wrap up an alpha umbilical session, make sure you conclude on a win, whether it's getting your dog to follow your lead from the living room to the kitchen or through the front door after a walk.
* With any training, whether it's umbilical or basic training like sit and stay, if you're not having success with the exercise you've been working on, go back to an exercise the dog can already do and get her to do it three times consecutively.
* As you continue doing umbilical training—or any of the other exercises I'll outline in this book—always end three consecutive wins with some praise. I recommend a good chest scrunch. In my opinion, that's the best physical method for praising your dog, particularly during the no talking period that I'll describe in the next chapter.
* The chest scrunch is easy: with your fingertips, massage your dog's chest for a few seconds, in the area between the top of her legs.

You can do umbilical training while you're at home, doing the laundry, making dinner, watching TV (with your dog on the ground, please, not on the couch with you), gardening outside or going for walks.

I discovered this technique when I started doggy daycare. I realized that if I didn't step around dogs, they'd quickly learn to get out of my way. They'd pay attention immediately and follow me around for hours—either literally or at least with their eyes. In other words, I had the dogs' undivided attention—such a cool thing. They would look up at me as if to say, "What's next?" It was clear that I had the alpha advantage. To keep *your* alpha advantage, make sure you move naturally and maintain confident body language. Your dog needs to learn that your physical movements can be powerful and that if he gets in the way, he might get hurt.

Clients often say, "I can't do that! It's abuse!" No, it's not. You are actually harnessing your dog's natural instinct to follow the pack leader. Remember that with domestic dogs, it's our job to provide them with that crucial alpha leadership. Otherwise, they might run into traffic and be killed. Or you'll have a rogue dog on your hands that could become aggressive and end up discarded or dead. How's that for abuse? Get with the program and embrace your leadership role. Remember that a dog is just an animal with forty-two sharp teeth until she's trained to become your pet.

I recommend doing umbilical training for two full weeks—every day for about two hours per day. But you don't have to drop all your own activities to do the work, and you don't have to spend two whole, consecutive hours with your dog. Some trainers say you have to dedicate one hour per day *exclusively* to training. I never tell my clients that kind of thing. It's better to incorporate training into your daily life, so you can break up the sessions. People sometimes ask, "What's the minimum amount of time I can spend on umbilical training?" which really says to me that they're starting off with low expectations—for themselves and for their pet. If you spend only two hours per day at home, spend that time on umbilical, no matter what else you're doing. The goal is to have your dog right at your side, watching you. It also gives you the chance to watch your dog, so you can stop her if she engages in any negative behaviours.

When you start umbilical training, an older dog that's been wearing the CEO title for years might struggle and manipulate from the start. Some of these CEOs might growl or refuse to budge. That simply means that in their eyes, you are weak and they're pretty sure that, eventually, you'll cave in. My advice is simple: don't cave! This is where patience and focus become essential. You'll be downright exhilarated when your rebel dog turns attentive and respectful. When that dog is looking up at you and she falls into sync with your movements, it means you're connected and in tune with each other's rhythm.

It's also a good idea to give umbilical refreshers every few months to keep you and your dog motivated to strive for an even better bond. Especially if you travel a lot without your dog, move house or are dealing with any sort of lifestyle changes.

———

CANINE SOCIAL SMARTS

*T*he human-dog bond is so important that the Family Dog Project in Budapest has compared it to the rich connection between a human mother and her infant. Healthy bonding has long-term payoffs, like improving the performance and cooperativeness of school-aged children. The researchers also found that dogs with higher-quality human bonds performed better in tasks and looked to their owners to help solve difficult problems. "This finding is often interpreted (in popular literature) as the 'pet dogs' being 'stupid' but this is not true!" the researchers declare. "In contrast, it means that dogs living in close relationship with their owner prefer to wait for the other to do the job for them, and only if this 'strategy' fails are they willing to solve the problem themselves. In other words dogs are very flexible in using social strategies."[17] The Budapest group also believes that dogs were domesticated for their "willingness to assume a subordinate role in their social group" and "follow social rules."[18]

This kind of research underscores the fact that domestic dogs depend on us for guidance and that it's our job as caregivers to take the lead role in developing this bond of trust.

The Power of Assertive Movement

Dogs are highly visual animals, and as I'll discuss in more detail in the next chapter, movement is a dog's first form of communication. They interpret our status as members of the social pack by the way we move, so you can raise your status in the dog's eyes simply by changing how you carry yourself. Your dog will interpret your disposition and state of mind through your body language. If you're slow, hesitant and anxious and look physically weak, they'll assume you're submissive and they'll feel the need to take charge. But if your body language is confident, dogs will get a clear message that you're holding the reigns, not just white-knuckling the leash. You don't have to be an athlete to train your dog, but to be really effective, you will need to get off your butt and move. You might wonder if this is true, given the dogs who work with disabled people, who are unable to move with great confidence or who cannot move much at all. These dogs are different. They're thoroughly trained before they start working as companion dogs, and they're cherry-picked for that kind of work because they have calm and mellow dispositions.

Dogs are highly adept at reading our human gestures as well, including the way we point, signal and move our eyes. Umbilical training intensifies that method of communication because it makes them even more tuned in to watching us.

This morning, I watched a client striding confidently along, with her dog walking right beside her with no leash; the dog kept looking at her and assessing that she was in control of the situation and could take care of him. That's a very powerful thing. The dog was saying, "I don't have to worry about anything. This person is leading me and has my safety in mind. I can just relax and enjoy the sunshine, fresh air and exercise."

Outdoor Umbilical

As I said earlier, you can do umbilical exercises at home, but please don't ignore the dog's need to get outdoor exercise. Doing outdoor umbilical is a great incentive for bonding with our dogs while everybody gets their needed exercise. As I mention in Chapter 5, I host outdoor group umbilical training sessions to help strengthen the agility of dogs and their two-legged owners and to get them mixing with other people and dogs in a variety of different places. The principle is pretty simple: walk, jog and run around outside with your dog leashed to your waist. I encourage you to do agility training, going for a run, weaving in and around objects or trees, during the umbilical phase. Once your dog is well exercised, she'll be much more willing to mellow out at home.

Chopper: Tyrannical King Turns Dog Prince

Chopper the bully golden retriever I mentioned at the beginning of the chapter came to our training program out of control. His owner, Heather, did the bulk of the training with him under our guidance. With an infant in the family, it was imperative for her to get Chopper to respect her as the boss. "Even total strangers could get him to do things I couldn't," says Heather. "After that first day of group training, I was so exhausted I cried. I thought, 'I'm never going back.' But that's when it really sunk in that I needed to step up to the plate and work hard. Otherwise, we'd lose Chopper."

Heather really dedicated herself to doing the full range of training that I'll be discussing in this book, but the alpha umbilical training was key. Of course, de-throning Chopper wasn't as simple as leading him around, but the alpha exercises were the foundation for all the exercises that followed. Umbilical exercises were critical for getting Heather not only to take control but also to establish a mutual level of respect and trust. "Chopper was finally listening to me. The more I moved, the more he followed, the more his tail wagged. He actually wanted to please me and seemed so much happier—we'd forgotten what a smart and fun dog he'd been before we'd lost control of him."

"On umbilical, Chopper paid attention immediately. It was amazing," says Dan. "We took away any opportunity he might have to lead us. If he tried to pull or get ahead of us, we'd give him a leash correction."

Leash Correction

I'll walk you through the leash correction method now. It's very simple, but highly effective, particularly in the early stages of umbilical training an unruly dog like Chopper. I have never seen leash correction fail. It is the best method for getting your dog's undivided attention. If your dog tries to strain against the leash at any point during the two weeks of umbilical training, use the leash correction method. The dog needs to understand that the leash is an extension of the trainer's power. It's all about managing the dog, not about being tough or physically abusive. As I pointed out earlier, a Martingale collar is designed to release quickly and won't hurt your dog, so that's the type of collar you should use. The correction is about being tough with yourself and clear with your directions. Follow these steps, whether you're walking around the house or outdoors:

* As soon as the leash strains and your dog starts to try to dictate movement, give the leash one quick pull upward. Your palm should be facing upward and your arm should be close to your side so you're using your core muscles to direct, instead of your shoulder. That way, if the dog flails, you're still in firm control.

* Make that one quick pull count. The fewer movements, the better. Don't go fishing and floundering with your arm so you have to keep yanking on the leash. It's imperative that you not condition a dog to any multiple commands. Think about it. If your dog bolts while off-leash at the park, by that third "Stop!" command, your dog could be dead. We don't want that.
* The goal is to make one concise and fluid movement, so the dog will understand that you mean business. Otherwise, you'll be confusing the dog; he'll have no clue as to what you want him to do. A nice, clean, crisp, controlled pull sends a clear message that you can handle the dog, and the dog will respond by looking to you for guidance.

Heather and Chopper attended my group umbilical classes for an entire year. Chopper was exposed to a huge number of dogs, and at first he'd growl or get anxious, but he never once lashed out. Once Chopper could see that Heather and Dan were in control, he didn't feel the need to be protective around other dogs. "He'd walk right by other dogs without any incidents," says Dan. "Our neighbours couldn't believe he was the same dog. Jordan is three years old now and can get him to sit and stay; he's just as much in control of Chopper as we are."

All in the Family

If you're like Heather and have an infant or toddler in the household, you're probably even more strapped for time than ever. Remember that if you feel stressed and overwhelmed, your dog will feel like that too. Dog training might seem impossible to wedge in alongside raising the kids and running the house, but believe me, in the long run, you'll save much more time, energy and expenses by rearing your dog to be well-behaved and relaxed. Umbilical is a great, easy way to assert alpha status while you juggle everything else: it frees up your hands to do chores, carry loads of laundry and cook, and it ensures that your dog is by your side so you don't have to worry about run-ins with the kids. It also provides your dog with a bit of physical and mental stimulation because you'll be doing so many different things with her—not to mention some much-needed attention at a time when she might be feeling neglected and anxious. At first you'll have to take extra care navigating in certain places, such as on stairs and slippery wood floors, so never carry your children while doing umbilical training and be particularly mindful when going down stairs, especially outdoor stairs that can ice up in cold weather. On dog walks umbilical is also a lot safer than tying the leash to the baby stroller—never do that no matter how small your dog is!

Everybody in the family can do umbilical training, even the kids *in some cases*. Start with the family adults, though, especially if you have a big dog or a dog that has developed behaviour issues or has characteristics that could make him dangerous (see the "Safeguarding Children" section in this chapter on page 70). And, of course, any children who work with dogs need to be old enough and responsible enough to understand the training principles, mature enough to follow the rules, free of behaviour issues themselves and strong enough to manage the particular dog in question. The dog must also have none of the issues described in the "Safeguarding Children" section. If there is even a remote possibility that the child or the dog could harm each other, the training must be left to adults.

Of course, the adults need to supervise all training involving their kids and be on the lookout for any warning signs that the dog or kids are getting tired and frustrated. If the dog seems distracted, pants or lies down or if his eyes get bloodshot or glassy, suspend training for the day. But whenever you wrap up training, make sure you end on a win, whether it's five paces or the entire length of the backyard with the dog following your lead. As the kids build up confidence and comfort, move outside for walks and then go on trips to the dog park.

Here's a test to see if your dog is ready to do umbilical with the kids, assuming the dog is not too physically difficult (e.g., too large) for the child to handle and does not have any of the issues described under the "Safeguarding Children" section (on page 70):

* With the dog on a leash, drape the handle of the leash across the top of your hand (but do not hold onto the leash in any way) and start walking.
* If the leash slips off because your dog has rushed ahead, you need to do more training before the kids get involved.

So many of my young clients have become star umbilical trainers. There's nine-year-old Mia, for instance. I met Mia when she was seven, and she took so well to umbilical training her own dog that I recently called her to help me with a Dalmatian whose parents claimed they couldn't manage him on walks. With my supervision, she stepped into the lead and that Dalmatian became calm and obedient almost immediately. How's that for proving the doubters wrong?

Mia's parents came to me when Jackson, their miniature golden doodle, was a six-month-old puppy who wasn't taking well to house training. (Note that Jackson the doodle is not to be confused with Jackson the Rottweiler, whom you'll meet in the next chapter.) "I was also potty-training my second daughter," says Jennifer, a busy stay-at-home mom. "Jackson was peeing and pooping all over the house. It was incredibly stressful, and at the end of the day, I was usually on the verge of tears." Jenn had tried puppy classes, but they were no help with house training or any other training for that matter. Then she heard me being interviewed on the radio and immediately called me up.

We started doing umbilical training right away. "I tiptoed around Jackson the first few times," Jenn admits. "But I knew I had to get it right and take control. Right away, I noticed a change in Jackson. He was paying attention to me, and the more time he spent on umbilical, the longer he could hold himself from going to the bathroom. It was the nicest, most stress-free two weeks I'd had in a long time." (See Chapter 9 for more step-by-step methods for house training.)

Jenn is the ideal client. She did her homework from the start, choosing a respectable breeder and seeking professional help with training. "We set up rules and boundaries with our kids, so why not with our dog?" she says. "Being 'nice' to your dog means being strict and devoted to training. Now Jackson's two, and he can go off-leash. Everyone always asks, 'What did you do to have such a great dog?' I tell them it was a whole lot of hard work."

———

Safeguarding Children

There are so many factors involved with training a dog to be safe and respectful with kids: the age of the kids, the age and size of the dog, whether the dog has been treat trained or has food-related aggressions, whether the dog is highly sensitized to sudden movements or high-pitched sounds like the wail of a baby, whether the dog likes to guard and is protective of a baby or small child in the family or whether the dog has obsessive tendencies, particularly with small animals.

Whatever the character of the dogs who need training, I like to compare them to high chairs. I know it sounds crazy, but hear me out. A dog can be a great asset for a family, helping kids learn to bond and empathize with others and also to play and have fun—but they can also be dangerous, especially if you leave them alone with the kids. The mix of high chair *and* dog can be downright deadly, especially with big dogs, dogs that are treated like vacuum cleaners and treat-trained dogs. A dog that's Hoovering up food crumbs under the high chair might accidentally bump it over. A treat addict might jump up at the child's food and toss the chair, and baby, right down onto the floor. We can avoid these potential disasters by, first and foremost, eliminating treats but also by carefully monitoring the dog's general behaviour before she starts mixing with kids. Does she become anxious or lash out at the sound of sudden noises or at the sight of awkward and unusual movements? If so, be extra vigilant and keep the dog away from crawling babies or a toddler learning how to walk. These teetering toddler cuties look harmless to us, but dogs might see their sudden movements as aggressive—and feel obliged to respond in kind.

You need to be extra-sentient when both dogs and kids

are around, teaching both species the rules of conduct. Your kids also need to understand that dogs feel pain just like people, so teach them how to pet a dog gently. As I'll discuss in more detail in the chapter about canine communication (Chapter 3), the dog might also tutor your kids on the rules by barking, growling or showing teeth. That doesn't necessarily mean your dog is about to eat your kid for breakfast; it may simply mean that he's saying, "Hey, this bugs me." It's the adult caregivers' job to take actions to eliminate the stressors that could bother the dog.

PARTY ON, DOG

We reward ourselves for hard work with time off to play, socialize and party. And dogs need to party sometimes too. The importance of these social interactions for dogs has been studied by scientists at the Family Dog Project in Budapest. "Social play represents one of the most complex interactions between two individuals," according to the experimenters, who found that play helped dogs develop skills like cooperation, conflict avoidance and reduced fearfulness and inhibition.[19]

The group observed dogs playing ball and tug games with their owners, with strangers and also with other dogs. They found that the dogs engaged more with humans than with other dogs, whether they knew the humans or not. And the dogs that had more play and socialization in their daily lives "were more likely to give up in competition" and follow "mutually accepted behaviour rules to avoid conflicts"—and they were more interactive and less possessive of toys than dogs that had less play time. Dogs exposed to less play were more likely to misunderstand play cues and show fear or avoidance behaviours. The researchers concluded that play games like tug and fetch didn't increase combative and competitive behaviour but instead enhanced the dogs' cooperative skills.

The researchers also found that human-dog play decreased a chemical called cortisol, which typically increases during stressful and combative situations. And within thirty minutes of play, they found that dogs buddied up to a new human friend.[20]

All Work and No Play

Don't forget to have fun while you're doing umbilical. Establishing alpha is serious business, but some people go too far by not having enough fun, and it shows in their sad-sack dogs. Break up any training sessions with some playtime time-outs. If you're too strict with training and don't allow your dog any time and space to play, you'll stifle the dog's potential. I also see this problem with some trainers and their dogs: the dog is treated like a working dog and isn't given permission to clock out once in a while. And as I said before, expecting perfection will bring trouble later on.

Once you've clearly established your alpha role, you'll be able to loosen up the reigns and go unleashed in so many ways. Off-leash training is the ultimate reward for both species. Peggy and Steve, the hard-working professionals mentioned in Chapter 1, eventually brought their "problem" dog, Rocky, to my Hustle Up school. The resulting investment in diligent and responsible training has paid off for everyone—to the point where Rocky's mom lets him take the lead sometimes. Peggy now trusts that she can follow Rocky, which makes him feel trusted, like an older sibling letting the younger one lead a walk through the woods. That simple act fulfills Rocky's need to be busy with a job as a lookout, overseeing the safety of others. It also allows him to prove to Peggy that he's not going to bolt away. That strengthens their bond.

The Mutt Rut

Routine might seem necessary for us humans with our fast-paced, time-strapped lifestyles, but rigid routines can actually cause negative dog behaviours. One of my clients had a strict schedule, and when the family happened to break that routine, they came home to a dog-trashed house. Another client was single for years, and when a new partner entered her life, the routine suddenly changed and the dog naturally pinned the change on the new family member, which caused resentment and jealousy issues that I'll talk about in greater detail in Chapters 6 and 7. The dog might just have been reacting to a change in exercise and feeding patterns, but it's best to avoid these potential alpha battles altogether by steering clear of schedules that are too strict. Consistency in training is crucial with dogs, but unvaried routine makes them inflexible to change and eventually bores them.

My clients sometimes confuse consistency with routine, and I have to stress that there's a big difference between the two. When I talk about consistency, I'm referring to the need to establish, maintain and expect good conduct and behaviour from your dog. Ditto for consistent boundaries, so your dog understands your household rules and knows what's allowed and what's off limits. (I'll get into more details about maintaining house rules in Chapter 6.) But it's also about training yourself—by sending consistent messages and being self-disciplined, focused, patient and motivated to work hard.

Our routines might seem necessary and innocent to us, so we think our dogs either accept them or are oblivious to them. Most canines don't have schedules as hectic as human timetables, but they're sponges, constantly dialing in to the subtle details to figure out what's going on; that's a good thing—as long as it's clear that you're in the driver's seat and that you will feed their need for stimulation (so they don't have to go looking for it somewhere else). Dogs that already wear the family pants are control freaks, so they look at any lapse in routine as an invitation to act out like divas.

I highly recommend that you do your best to avoid putting your dog into a routine with anything: feeding, bathroom, bedtime, walk time, going to a specific dog park at a specific time every week. It's always best to mix it up because that keeps your dog on her paws, so to speak, and allows her to be resilient and adaptive to change.

Alpha with Everything
Alpha training your dog is the most critical first step in developing and nurturing a strong, trusting bond with your animal. Here are a variety of ways you can establish and maintain the leader rank with your dog. (Some of them have been described in this chapter; others are mentioned for the first time here or detailed in later chapters.)

* To start your dog off in the right way (or to correct a dog who acts up), do umbilical training for at least two hours every day for two weeks.

* Don't talk to your dog at all during the two-week period of initial umbilical training, particularly if you have already talked to your dog a great deal and he has become desensitized to your verbal commands. Use movement, snapping and hand gestures to command your dog's attention. (See Chapter 3 for more information about these.) When you do start talking to your dog, always speak in a firm, calm voice and refrain from using high-pitched tones, which dogs interpret as a sign of weakness or even pain.

* Always assume the lead position whenever you're with your dog. Harness your dog's natural instincts to follow the pack leader by teaching him that your movements have power. That way, he'll get in sync with your rhythm, not the other way around. Only after a trusting bond is absolutely secure between you and your dog can you let the dog lead occasionally, but even that should be done only rarely.

* Use the leash correction method I outlined in this chapter to control your dog's movements and to correct bad behaviours.

* After the two weeks of umbilical training, never let your dog dictate movement by pulling on the leash at any point—unless you are doing a quick leash correction.

* Always feed your dog *after* you've eaten.

* Never let your dog sit on the human furniture.

* Provide your dog with basic training: sit, stay, come, stop. (See Chapter 4.) This training will not only street-proof your dog and teach her to respect and follow your commands; it will also feed her need for

structure and cultivate her skills.

* Turf the food treats as "rewards" and use positive rewards like physical exercise, play and thinking games, which stimulate the dog mentally but allow you to maintain control of the action.
* Expose your dog to a mix of activities so she knows she can trust you as the pack leader in a wide variety of settings and situations. (See Chapter 5 for my agility, street-safety and off-leash training exercises.)
* Teach your dog the house rules, so he learns to appreciate and respect your possessions. (See Chapter 6.)
* Interrupt and correct bad behaviours immediately. (See Chapters 4 and 6 for my methods, which mimic dogs' disciplinary techniques.)
* Patience-train your dog to curb insecurities and separation anxiety. (See Chapter 7.)
* Be consistent with your training, but do your best to avoid strict routines. That way, your dog won't become complacent or bored and will always look to you for direction because he won't be sure of what's going to happen next.

CHAPTER THREE

Dog Speak

HARNESSING CANINE COMMUNICATION METHODS TO ENHANCE INTERSPECIES RELATIONS

MYTH: If your dog barks or growls incessantly, she is dangerous.

REALITY: Barking is simply one method that dogs use to communicate their various needs and emotions. It's your job to figure out what your dog is trying to tell you. If your dog barks at everything that moves, she's probably bored, insecure and in some way attempting to assert alpha status. Dogs typically become territorially aggressive only when we neglect their primary needs.

Learning to Speak Rottweiler

Jackson, a 110-pound Rottweiler, was a complete basket case when I started training him at six months of age. He was totally disobedient, which is unacceptable for any dog, but especially a big, strong galloot like Jackson. He actually has a very sweet and gentle temperament, but he barked a lot because he had insecurity issues and needed to learn that he could trust his owner to be the boss. Jackson could have gone down the wrong path without a good owner like Harvey, who started dog training a week after he inherited Jackson from another bachelor who had raised Jackson without rules, boundaries or basic dog training. The primary goal of my program for Harvey and Jackson was to cultivate a bond of trust between the two of them and get them communicating in a way that both species understood. That way, they would have a strong foundation to start a successful training program.

"Jackson felt like he had the run of the house," says Harvey. "He barked all the time, would try to bolt outside whenever he had the chance, and he had no respect for me and my possessions. I knew I had to be the boss right away and lay down strict rules, but I had no clue how to communicate with him. When I told him not to do anything, he just ignored me."

Communication between Harvey and Jackson was like an Abbott and Costello Who's-on-first? comedy routine. Jackson had no clue what Harvey was saying to him. That gentle giant needed a lot of training, but I loved working with him. The key factor with a dog that has assumed the stressful role of family alpha—no matter what his size and strength—is to provide a well-rounded training program that stimulates the dog's muscles between the ears and harnesses his primary methods of communication: physical movement. Based on my experience with Jackson and other canines, I'll discuss the best ways to communicate verbally with your dog. I'll also talk about why dogs bark excessively and provide exercises to curb that barking. I'll top it all off with a crash course in canine communication, so you can interpret what your dog's specific barks, growls and body language mean.

First, I want you to think about the way dogs communicate with each other. How often do you see two dogs talking to each other verbally? Rarely, right? When they meet up, dogs typically wag their tails, pump out their chests and sniff the bums to say hello. They don't often say, "Hey, George, how ya doin' today? Didja pick up the daily news on that bench?" They're rarely yabbering at each other. And we should shut up more often too—at least with our dogs. We yap at them far too much, and in too many cases, our talking is so repetitive that dogs tune us out. Much of our talking is also emotionally overwrought, thus revealing—too much about our feelings.

Notice how many professional poker players clam up when they have a big hand or they're bluffing? At times like this, other players try to engage them in inane chatter to gauge their emotions from their tone of voice. Other players wear sunglasses or sit on their hands so their eyes and gestures won't give them away. With dogs, talking when you're stressed in any way is like putting all your cards on the table in a poker game. Whether your dog has alpha tendencies or not, she will read your emotional tone as a weakness and either feel the need to take the reigns or become anxious and insecure. Verbal commands can be very effective, and they're especially necessary in safeguarding dogs when they're off-leash and in urban settings, but less is always more; the best way to communicate verbally is to use a firm but calm tone and articulate your words clearly.

Say you go to France. Even if you don't know much

French, if you can say a few simple words, like *bonjour* and *merci beaucoup* and *au revoir*, people will accept you more than if you don't try at all. Ditto for your dog. Why should your dog even try to accept you if you don't attempt to understand her language? We need to take the time to observe how they communicate with each other with movements, actions, gestures and body language and then learn to harness these methods of communication to our advantage, particularly while we're doing basic training. We can also read their body movements and use our own movements and gestures to create a dialogue that they'll able to appreciate and that will command their attention.

Of course, dogs like to talk; the extent simply depends on each dog's unique personality. They use their voices quite effectively to articulate their feelings, so we need to familiarize ourselves with the tones they use when they bark and growl—and more importantly, we need to understand why they're doing what they're doing. Dogs typically bark excessively only when they're bored and understimulated.

We can also interpret dogs' moods by being attentive to their movements and their body positions. When people start paying attention to that language, as well as putting a muzzle on their own human barking, they'll have a richer relationship with their dogs.

Zip It Already

One of the first things I tell a client to do is to cease and desist talking to the dog altogether for two weeks—at the same time that they're doing umbilical. That's very difficult for many people because they're so used to talking to their four-legged friends. They think they have to talk to the dog to strengthen their bond, when the opposite is really the case.

Within hours, if not immediately after you zip it, you'll likely notice that your dog is looking at you and following you around more often. However, dogs who've been exposed to total chatterboxes might start to act depressed or needy over the next four days. That's exactly the reaction you want, so stay strong and keep your mouth zipped. Don't cave! The dog is paying attention to you, which is actually a natural state for dogs. You're showing that you're not looking for the dog anymore, and your dog will start looking for you. It's magic. Huge power.

This is especially helpful for women who struggle with getting their dogs to pay attention because their wonderful, soft voices unfortunately don't always make canines sit up and take notice. I have many women clients who have a much tighter bond with their dogs than their husbands do. But the man of the family has the bigger, deeper voice, and this makes the dog respond to him with more immediacy. The wife will say, "He doesn't listen to me. He only pays attention to my husband. It's like I'm the substitute teacher. Then the principal shows up, and all of a sudden, the dog smartens right up."

Women can help de-fuse these conflicts by developing signals and gestures, by snapping or clapping and by using decisive and assertive movements with their dogs. It's not always a negative thing if a dog acts playful or even gets a bit mischievous with his female owner. Busy moms, especially, are constantly on the go, and it's hard for the dog not to pick up on that energy. But as long as the behaviour isn't really negative and clear lines have been drawn firmly, allowing the dog to be playful can really enrich the bond and the level of mutual respect between owner and pet.

Tone It Down

Another benefit to keeping your mouth shut is that if you've had a bad day and you come home and speak to the dog, she'll pick up on your tension as if you were an open book. The dog interprets our different tones—from aggressive sounds to baby talk, and an alpha dog will use these as ammo to notch up his power. Calm, submissive dogs, on the other hand, will become confused and stressed out. Either way, your dog will start to act out and then your emotions will escalate as a result. If you baby-talk at the dog, saying something like "Oooh, baby, I missed you today" and then "Oh, please be nice to Daddy," the dog will be overwhelmed by your emotional messages and act out. It's a vicious cycle that can be prevented by keeping your mouth zipped—or at the very least by stifling your emotions and faking a calm voice.

Dogs have much better hearing than we humans, so if you scream at your dog all the time (or even a fair bit of the time), imagine how much pain that would inflict on their psyches. Be particularly respectful of dogs' keen hearing after they have been spayed or neutered. Those Elizabethan collars (the cones vets put on dogs' heads so they won't scratch their incisions) act like satellite dishes, amplifying noises. Sure dogs can look hilarious in those contraptions, but how would you like to convalesce from surgery, surrounded by the noise of people laughing at you like hyenas?

————

BABY TALK

*P*eople baby-talk with high voices because it makes them feel good—or because they're trying to emulate the maternal role of a pup's mother. But a mother of pups doesn't communicate verbally in a high pitch. Her movements are softer and gentler, but she's firm with her growls and barking. Baby-talk is the opposite of what she does with her litter. The only time you hear really high pitches from dogs is if they've been hurt or if they're wrestling and they say, "Ouch" with a little yip or squeak to show that you've crossed a boundary.

Rude Human Barking

You're at the dog park. How much noise do you really hear? It's the *people* making the most noise, and they're typically barking like crazy at their dogs. The most common human barking is used to try to make the dog come back to the owner. Two Legs yells, "Charlie, come here!" If Charlie respects Two Legs as boss, he'll hustle back pretty quick. If not, Charlie will just ignore the verbal command and continue enjoying his cocktail party. Two Legs tries again with more intensity: "*Charlie*, get over here!" Charlie might look over at his owner and say, "Whatever. I've got dogs to see and butts to smell." But Two Legs keeps yelling with greater intensity, and the more highly charged those verbal commands become, the more Charlie tunes out. Now the owner is in full freak-out mode, having a total tantrum, but the dog couldn't care less.

If this happens to you, it could mean that your dog doesn't

get enough exercise and time to socialize with other dogs. However, if you've been fulfilling these basic doggy needs and you still have dog park stand-offs, you probably have an alpha problem on your hands that could escalate to serious behaviour issues.

Mixed Messages

Many dog owners fluctuate between baby-talking to their dogs and lashing out at them like drunken bullies—sometimes within a period of minutes. Imagine how confused you'd be if a person hugged you and then screamed in your face. You'd either shrink in terror every time they tried to hug you again or you'd get the heck away from them immediately. And just because dogs don't really have option number 2 doesn't make your erratic behaviour any more acceptable.

Flip-flopping back and forth between one extreme behaviour and another isn't acceptable for dogs, and it shouldn't be allowed among humans either. Dogs should be able to expect predictable, rational behaviours from you as much as you should expect them from dogs.

Actions Speak Louder: Dog Linguists Dez and Max

As I mentioned earlier, my dogs Dez and Max taught me so many wonderful things about canines. One of the most critical lessons was to understand why they were barking and help them fulfill the needs they were trying to articulate.

One day, I was driving along the highway and there was a bunch of cattle in the ditch up ahead. Dez and Max started to bark with the same sort of "boundary alert" tone that they used when kids horsed around too much. I thought they might be saying, "Those cattle are on the wrong side of the fence." So I stopped the car and let the two of them out. Sure enough, they immediately started herding the cows back around the fence. It took only about twenty minutes to do something that met a strong need in them (and helped the farmer), and it was a simple way to pay them back for being such outstanding companions.

After that, I made a point of giving those two dogs work whenever the opportunity arose. Living in Alberta, that wasn't too challenging, since it's Canada's cattle heartland. Once, they helped moved cattle off a golf course fairway, and another time, they herded twenty-two horses two miles along a highway, with rush-hour traffic speeding by. The more freedom I gave those dogs, the more they respected me and followed my commands when I needed them to be safe and well behaved. They were especially respectful in off-leash situations, which is the ultimate way to reward a dog for good behaviour.

I know that not all of you can expose your dogs to the kind of activities they might crave. And as I underlined in the last chapter, you certainly shouldn't be a slave to your dog's every whim. But if your dog starts barking at all the kids at a birthday party, tries to herd them into a corner or barks after placing his favourite fetch ball at your feet, only to be ignored, that dog is simply saying, "Hey, throw me *some* kind of bone, please!" You might not be able to drop everything pronto, but if you bark right back at him and continue to ignore those needs, nobody wins.

Conversations with Jackson the Rottweiler

Jackson's training program began with a strict no talking policy for two weeks while Harvey was doing umbilical training with him. As I pointed out in the last chapter, this approach primes dogs to follow your lead and pay attention to your *body movements* and *body language* instead of your voice. This creates a literal bond that teaches the dog to trust you in the lead role and curbs the potential of your messages getting lost in translation. It's frustrating for both species to misunderstand each other, and this makes training so much more challenging—and sometimes downright impossible—especially with dogs that have never been given any structure or rules.

Getting back to Jackson . . . You could talk with him until you were blue in the face, telling him to sit or stop barking, but he'd just look up at you with his big brown eyes as if to say, "Huh? I don't get it. Talk to the paw. I'm going over here to have a stimulating conversation with this stick." When something like that happens, you might assume that the dog is simply too stupid to learn anything, when he is actually giving the obvious message—in his own language—that a stick, a ball or a darting squirrel is better company than you.

"The umbilical was critical," says Harvey. "And combined with the no talking rule, Jackson was always looking at me for leadership and direction. That curbed his barking tendencies almost immediately because he knew I was in control of the situation. If he tried to break any rules—barking, chewing, tugging at the leash—I'd be right there to interrupt and correct his actions."

These interruption and correction techniques are effective because dogs can easily understand them: quick, fast actions that catch dogs off-guard and focus their attention on their owners. (See Chapter 4 for detailed instructions.)

"The goal was to teach Jackson that certain behaviours weren't cool," says Harvey. "He actually learned quickly and immediately started looking to me for leadership. Dogs communicate so much with body language, so he responded really well to my actions and gestures. When I wanted him to sit, I'd put him on a piece of carpet and give the leash one quick pull upward to get his butt down. (See Chapter 4 for detailed instructions about sit-stay training.) At first I could only get him to sit for a few seconds before he started barking and going nuts, but as soon as he started to move, I'd pull the leash up again and snap my finger. We did that every night until he could sit for an hour while I did other things. As soon as he got up, I'd grab onto his collar and place him back on the carpet. The key is consistency and never letting him win by ignoring my commands. It was a battle of wills, but I didn't give Jackson any rope. We practised every night and on weekends, and by the end of the two weeks of umbilical and no talking training, I just had to snap to get him to sit, and I'd push my hand down toward the ground to get him to lie down."

SNAP, CLAP AND POINT: NON-VERBAL COMMANDS

Snapping and hand signals are great non-verbal communication methods. You could also use clapping and pointing or whatever gestures you like, but just as in the case of the leash correction I described in the last chapter, the goal is to make the gesture once and make it count. Don't start acting like a mime artist doing a street show. Keep your signal or gesture simple, concise and consistent to prevent misinterpretations.

The Postie Never Rings Twice

Another priority was getting Jackson to stop barking like a belligerent maniac. The best way to do that was to feed his need for exercise and socialization with a lot of umbilical walks. But first I had to get Harvey to understand exactly why Jackson barked at everything that moved—especially the mail carrier: an understimulated dog's worst enemy.

Barking at the postie is the most common way dogs exhibit their boredom—and drive their owners nuts. Though people usually assume the problem is with the dog; it almost always is not! I get complaints all the time about dogs barking like crazy at the postman or postwoman from the window, then grabbing for the mail when it comes through the slot and shredding it up as if the mail itself was a sworn enemy. Sometimes, I have to laugh at this bad doggy behaviour. It actually reveals some pretty cool things about the way dogs think and act.

If a dog isn't getting enough exercise and mental stimulation, he starts to make up his own games. It might be obsessing over squirrels in the yard or the cat on the balcony across the street—or if the dog's pent up in the house all day, it could mean going into attack mode every time someone passes the house, particularly if that person dares to walk right up the front steps and lob something into the house—and has the nerve to do it *every single day!* When bored dogs shred mail and attack mail carriers, they're assuming the household alpha role, and for dogs, that means protecting the house.

Put yourself in Jackson's mindset for a second. It's 11 a.m. So far his day's been a complete bore ever since Harvey loped off to work. For a bit of distraction, he flosses his teeth with Harvey's running shoes, then heads for his corner office at the front window. Not much action out there, but he's got a bit of work done, barking at a couple of cars and a pedestrian with a baby stroller that dared to go past. Every single time, he manages to scare off these interlopers!

Oh yeah, I'm top dog, thinks Jackson, admiring his reflection in the windowpane. But he knows the biggest challenge still lies ahead. Periodically, he checks his dog watch to monitor how long it will be before his arch-nemesis shows up: the blue devil with the giant pouch slung over his shoulder. Where is that two-legged creep! Late *again.* The tension mounts as the minutes tick by. *Ohmygawd,* there's the villain, finally, across the street! Ruff, ruff, ruff! Why does he always play this weird game of up the walkway, down the walkway? Ruff, ruff, ruff. Aha, he's gone, but he's such a sneaky bastard he'll probably be back. Now, if I scrunch my enormous snout right up against the window, I'll see him coming up the sidewalk next door before he sees me. Where the heck is he? Oh, just as I suspected, he's back. Ruff, ruff, ruff. Oh, it worked again! He's gone again. Wait! Dammit, he's back, and now he's approaching *my* property line. Ruff, ruff, snarl, growl, ruff. How dare you come up my walkway! Ruff, growl, snarl. Oh, there's the mailbox cover clanking. Who does he think he is? Better lay it on thicker. Ruff, growl, ruff! There he goes. It worked! Ah, another successful day crushing my number 1 enemy. But, boy, how I'd love to get my fangs into that guy one day. I bet he'd be delicious. *Whatever,* now I'll have a snooze until the school kids parade home for lunch. Maybe the FedEx dude or the pizza delivery guy will show later . . .

So do you think Jackson feels he's succeeded in protecting the house? Totally. Every day. And people wonder why their dogs always go into attack mode when they see the postie. Once the game has been going on for a while, when your dog finally comes face-to-snout with the postie, it's like she's been a cat trying to get the goldfish but there's a lid on the tank and then all of a sudden, the goldfish is on the table flopping around. Your dog's an opportunist, and over time, she's become increasingly cocky, intense and aggressive. It's a game of cat and mouse. The dog is saying, "Dammit! I need to protect the house." And if that's the only entertainment the dog is getting, well, what do you expect?

Remember that, in your dog's mind, the annoying and seemingly bizarre habit of mad barking is actually fulfilling her craving to be a successful member of your home pack. She thinks she's doing a good job protecting the home while you're away. To get her out of the habit, you have to start wearing the pants in the family. Own up to the leadership position so your pooch can relax, take the backseat or, when you're not home, do what well-balanced dogs typically do in such circumstances: sleep.

I'm not saying that every single well-behaved dog will be completely uninterested in the humans who enter their worlds. If Dez saw the postie, she'd glance up and think *Whatever* and then get back to her own world. Max was more of a busybody. He liked to say hello to people and would even escort the postie down the walkway. That was rather hospitable, I thought. How many of us Two Legs take such a benevolent interest in our posties? When one of my clients was having problems with her dog pestering a postie, I suggested that she ask the postie if she and her dog could walk with him along part of his route. He was game for that and eventually even did a bit of umbilical with the dog. But how many posties have the time for such activities?

Remember that this dog-versus-postie dilemma is a potential lawsuit waiting to happen if your dog's dream of meeting the postie in the flesh ever does come true. If you live in an apartment, you might not have to deal with mail carriers, but an understimulated high-rise-dwelling dog might bark every time she hears the ding of an elevator or neighbours, couriers and cleaning personnel coming and going.

Do your best to prevent a close encounter of the fang-bearing kind by making sure you're meeting your basic obligations to the dog. That way your pooch won't turn into a rogue. And to be aware of the seriousness of the matter, remember that nobody is truly safe from rogue dogs. So when dog owners are ill equipped to manage their pets, they need to understand that they're putting their neighbours and a lot of professionals in potential danger. Some owners will say, "Oh, I don't want to hurt the dog. If I correct him, I'll hurt his feelings." But it's okay to destroy someone else's life? As I'll discuss in Chapters 4 and 6, you have to interrupt and correct a dog when she becomes territorially aggressive and teach her that there are specific rules and boundaries.

When Harvey realized that Jackson had got into the bad habit of barking at everything through no fault of his own (we can blame his previous owner for that), he also started to understand what Jackson's barking meant. To bust that, the top priority was to give Jackson enough exercise, physically and mentally, and to expose him to a variety of sights and sounds. (If you're doing all of these things and your dog is still barking like crazy, he might have a more serious behavioural issue like separation anxiety. I'll provide more strategies for curbing anxiety-related barking in Chapter 7.)

With Harvey now dictating their movements, Jackson was learning to follow Harvey's lead. That strengthened their bond, and I also recommended outdoor activities that made Jackson more mellow at night.

Re-Introducing Verbal Commands

After the two-week umbilical and no talking period, Harvey introduced verbal commands. After all the silence, the impact of his words were now much stronger and took Jackson by surprise, which again focused his attention. Harvey would say, "No noise," in a firm, deep tone whenever Jackson got to feeling he had to step in and play alpha by barking. "If Jackson barked, I'd give him a leash correction," says Harvey. "I did the same thing outdoors. I'd tie him to a tree and start walking away. At first he was really nervous and would let out these high-pitched barks, so I would immediately turn back and say, "No noise." Then I'd gradually build up the distance until he was able to sit quietly." (I'll walk you through this exercise in Chapter 7.)

"The whole process of training took about six months," says Harvey. "But now Jackson knows the rules. He doesn't trash my stuff and he rarely barks. Some dogs like to use their voices, like his pal Rudy, my own dog. But Jackson's actually a pretty quiet dog. He still lets off a bark when the mailman shows up, but I just say, 'Okay, Jackson,' to acknowledge the comment. If he barks again, I say, 'Okay, no noise.'"

"Now Jackson's off-leash more than he's leashed," says Harvey. "We respect each other and have a great relationship. Jackson is so easygoing and mellow now that he trusts my leadership and knows how to be well behaved. It took a lot of patience and consistency, but the payoff is having a dog that I can take everywhere and trust to be around everyone, kids especially."

Jackson is a pleasure to hang out with now. He has a great friendship with Rudy, and their bond is really fascinating because 15-pound Rudy is always the top dog in that relationship. Jackson is a 110-pound sweetheart. I often call on him to help me train other dogs, especially aggressive ones. He'll stand his ground, but he never fights back.

Listen to the Body Language: Tails, Necks, Heads and Ears

Curbing our human talk also helps us focus on observing dogs' movements and body language. Dogs learn a lot about us through our body language, and we can do the same with them—focusing especially on their tails, necks, heads and ears.

There are a lot of theories floating around about tail, ear and other body positions, but there's really no gold standard for any of these; all dogs are different and have unique ways of expressing themselves. I'm going to give you some general advisories, but take them with a good dose of salt, since your dog's body language might be quite different. Tail positions can be a good gauge of a dog's emotional state, though I've met more than my share of happy dogs who didn't or couldn't wag their tails. If the tail is upright and swaying slightly at the tip, the dog is likely confident and relaxed. When the entire tail starts to sway back and forth, the dog might be feeling sociable and ready to be engaged with other people and dogs. If a dog has his tail tucked underneath his belly, he might be nervous, stressed out or feeling self-conscious. If his tail is sticking straight out and perhaps moving slightly, he might want to mix, but he's feeling somewhat cautious and hesitant. If his tail is extended but rigid, he might be feeling tense, but this may simply be an indication that he's a dog that likes to guard. It's not necessarily a sign of danger. Chances are his tail will start wagging, but we might want to be extra-attentive to any potential danger that he might be picking up on.

Head and neck positions can also be revealing. If your dog holds her head high, she might be feeling confident. She might drop her neck toward her shoulders, and if her body is relaxed, this might mean she's open to mixing. But if she extends her neck, she could be on the defensive and might even become aggressive. Be watchful of a dog who tries to put his head and neck on top of another dog or a small person. That's an alpha position. It might simply be his way of establishing doggy rank before engaging in play, and if the other dog is very submissive, he might back off. If the other dog is willing to engage, she might spin in a half-circle, which says, "Okay, let's play, but on an equal footing. Don't try to dominate me." At that point the dogs' necks will relax and they'll start to play. But if the other dog shortens her neck, it could mean a dog fight is imminent, so you might have to act fast to extract your dog from the situation. In Chapter 5, I'll talk about how important it is for your dog to have a social life with other dogs and to know the rules of dog engagement, so you can avoid dog-dog conflicts.

Ear movement is also an interesting form of dog expression. Some dogs will pin their ears back tight to the head not only when they're aggressive but also when they're irritated. Jackson's ears go back, kind of like a facial flinch, if you baby-talk to him. He's not going to lash out, but he's saying, "Geez, that's annoying." Some dogs won't move their ears at all in situations like this, though, so you won't be able to read them that way.

Despite the guidelines I've just given, it's not wise to read the emotions and movements of our individual dogs based on any stuffy formula. Get to know your dog's body movements in a variety of different situations—around sudden, loud noises or movements, upon greeting other dogs and people (while leashed at first), around small children—before you make any guesstimates about their emotions and behaviours. If you don't have a good gauge for reading your dog in situations that might result in a dog fight or cause your dog to lash out, keep her leashed up while you introduce her to a variety of different stimuli and scenarios. You can only really get to know your dog's personality by introducing her to new situations.

HI-TECH DOGSPEAK

*D*og researchers are using computer technologies to interpret specific types of dog barks. The Family Dog Project in Budapest used a computer to classify over six thousand barks. Forty-three per cent of the time, the computer could correctly classify the barks, a percentage that most humans would be unable to reach.[21]

In Brazil scientists taught a mongrel dog named Sofia to communicate her desires—to be fed, walked, petted and given toys—by using a keyboard with simple symbols.[22] Maybe in the future, there will be a doggy computer in every home, but it's unlikely that dogs will send out most of their messages electronically. The Brazilian researchers found that 87 per cent of the time, Sofia used body language such as gazing and movement to indicate what she wanted. This supports the idea that you don't need a lot of sophisticated equipment to figure out what your dog wants; you just need to pay attention to his cues.

Canine Interpreter

Dogs bark and growl from their throats, chests or bellies. The place where a particular sound originates will indicate the dog's state of mind. When they use their throats and chests, they're rarely expressing a negative state of mind, though they might be sending out warning signs that could escalate to the point that they growl from their stomachs, and this means they've become aggressive. In that case, there's no time to react.

When the dog is speaking from her throat, she might be sending out an early warning sign. She might be saying that she's starting to feel the urge to go to the bathroom or that somebody's coming to the door. But she might just be telling you she likes something. For instance, if her belly is being scratched, she might just be saying that it feels good. Dogs also communicate with each other by throat growling, but that doesn't mean they're expressing aggression or conflict.

When it comes to warning growls, dogs talk from the chest. A growl like that could mean "I need to go to the bathroom, *now!*" Or if the kids are pestering the dog, he might be saying, "Enough already." Many people will freak out when that happens, assuming the dog is going to bite the kid. But that's not true at all. When a mom is with her puppies, she'll growl from her chest instead of from her throat, using a deeper tone to tell a certain puppy that it's breaking a rule, such as straying too far from the litter. A dog might also growl from the chest during play, and as the physical communication increases, so will the verbal communication, but neither of these growling scenarios is a sign of aggression.

A chest-growling dog might also be giving a warning like this: "Don't come into my corner! I have fear-aggression issues." If you then continue to encroach on her comfort zone, she'll possibly show teeth. That's not a bad thing. In fact, I encourage it because it's a good advance warning sign. At least, if you see that happening and you know it's a warning sign, you won't be blindsided by a dog attacking you. But what do we do with the information a growl gives us? Do we continue pushing the boundaries? Or acknowledge it and respond in a polite manner by backing the heck away?

If a dog's sending warning signs about something we're doing, the best thing to do is to cease and desist with whatever is making the dog uncomfortable. If the troublemaker is another dog or someone else's child and you can't control their actions, simply remove your dog from the situation. If you can't do that, then do your best to put distance between your dog and the offending party.

So far, the growls I've described have been relatively harmless. But when a dog growls from the pit of her stomach, she's no longer friendly. You won't have time to think, "I wonder what . . ." The dog has already resolved the situation in her mind and will attack—or she might just attack and growl from her stomach as she's launching her offensive. You have to be very alert to the earlier signs and act quickly to ensure that the dog doesn't escalate to that type of behaviour. If small children are near the dog, always be right there, supervising them, so you can step in when the dog starts sending out warning signs.

The Sound of Music

Like people, every dog differs in the amount they like to vocalize. Some are chatty and others are more reserved. Every dog's voice also has a unique sound: some are higher and some are lower. I know male dogs with high "girly" voices and female dogs with lower tones. Rocky, Peggy and Steve's Australian shepherd, lets out a hilarious high scream when you throw a stick for him to fetch. My dog, Rudy the Schnoodle, has a high pitch, too, and Dez could hurt your ears with her voice. Max had a very deep growl, and I sometimes encouraged him to use it. There was the time, for example, when I was at a drive-thru late at night and a sketchy dude started approaching the window. I just said, "Max, handle this." He turned and let out his deep, dominating bark, and the guy bolted immediately.

My dogs will sometimes bark to tell other dogs to be quiet, quit misbehaving in the vehicle or cut the rambunctious play. They also bark when kids jump on my couch, saying, "Boundary alert! Get the heck off, you brats!"

One dog buddy of mine loves blues music, and he'll howl and sing along to it. Dez was like that with all sorts of music or even when I'd say, "Ayooh." Rudy likes to sing sometimes too. And sometimes sirens will trigger a dog to howl.

Because canines have such heightened hearing, we need to be respectful of the volume and frequency of our own human sounds. You might love heavy-metal music turned up to eleven, but your dog is registering it at a much higher volume. The same goes for TV, especially with people who are hard of hearing. Some of my clients will leave the TV or music on all day while they're at work because they think it keeps their dog company. But does your dog really enjoy a constant stream of sound for eight to twelve hours? That could be downright annoying. If there's a lot of white noise in their lives, such as if you live in an apartment with thin walls or somewhere with a lot of street traffic, you might want to play music to curb those background sounds, but remember that TV and radio commercials are often louder and sometimes much more abrasive than the programs. Be considerate of these factors and please don't let a TV or stereo become a surrogate for true forms of mental and physical stimulation.

While I'm at it, I must add that there are snake-oil sales-people out there hawking dog music and videos as a method of *training* dogs, curbing their barking or getting them to relax and go to sleep. In my opinion, dogs will relax and sleep only if they're tired—and they're not going to be tired if they're not getting enough exercise.

Dogs should be allowed to vocalize their feelings, just like us. Even when they're driving us crazy, they're saying things we need to listen to. And communication can be brilliant if we take the time to figure out what they're saying and why they're saying it.

Recap: Dogspeak

The best method for communicating and bonding with your dog is to use movement, gestures and action as your primary interspecies language, whether you're teaching your dog the necessary skills to get along in the human world, giving your dog the physical exercise he needs or establishing and maintaining the house rules of conduct through interruption and correction techniques. Here's the checklist of effective techniques for healthy interspecies communication:

* Don't talk to your dog while you're doing the initial two weeks of umbilical training. By combining these two methods of engagement, your dog will be focusing attention on you and she'll be willing to follow your lead. You'll also become more observant of your dog's unique body language, so you can understand how to read her mood in a variety of different situations.

* Harness your dog's natural understanding of movement and body language as a foundation for teaching your dog the rules of engagement.

* After the two-week no talking period, use verbal commands sparingly and always use a calm, clear firm tone, so your words have heightened impact. Never coo, baby-talk or scream at your dog.

* Become familiar with the ways and reasons why your dog barks and growls. Allow your dog to express himself verbally and do your best to respond to those vocalizations appropriately.

* Provide your dog with her basic doggy needs—physical and mental stimulation—to ward off boredom and territorial insecurities that can lead to anxiety and aggressive behaviours.

CHAPTER FOUR

Basic Dog Training

TECHNIQUES THAT DOGS RESPECT VERSUS INDUSTRY FADS

MYTH: Treats are the most effective and "gentle" tool for dog training.

REALITY CHECK: Food rewards don't train dogs how to respect your leadership and get along in the real world. They often cause a whole range of negative behaviours, including food and territory-related aggressions. Dogs shouldn't view us as vending machines; they should see us as capable, trustworthy caregivers.

Trick-or-Treating Rocky

Rocky, the eleven-and-a-half-year-old Australian shepherd we first met back in Chapter 1, is a phenomenal dog now, but he was a complete mess when I met him when he was four. His parents, Peggy and Steve, weren't negligent owners; they sought out professional training for Rocky when he was a puppy, but the dog trainers they hired used treats. "Treats worked well during the indoor training sessions and for a week or so afterwards," says Peggy. "But Rocky would always up the ante and turn the tables on us. He's a strategic thinker, so he'd always end up outsmarting us."

The more treats Rocky got, the more disobedient he became—because they elevated his alpha status and his capacity to manipulate. He didn't act out at home, but as soon as he got outside, he turned freakazoid. Inside, his treats were things like pieces of dried meat, but in the great outdoors, he found much more tantalizing rewards—squirrels, bees, cyclists—and if his highly tuned senses got wind of those, he'd be off like a shot, chasing down whatever it was. When it became glaringly obvious that the treats weren't working, some trainers simply said Rocky couldn't be trained, and others offered only prong or choke collars. None of those trainers showed Rocky's parents any other methods for gaining control over their dog so that he could function safely and happily in the real world. As the years ticked by, Rocky had less and less respect for his parents, and he'd been taught no skills for following even the simplest commands effectively, such as when to sit, stay, come or stop.

"You could only depend on the treats *some* of the time, because Rocky would always decide whether he'd play the treat game or not," says Steve. "The bottom line was that treats were just another game for him. They were a total bust. We knew enough to know that dogs need to get something out of their relationships with humans, but treats were just bribes, which he could take or leave. The trainers gave us no skills that would help us understand Rocky. We felt as if we had no options left; no one could teach us."

In this chapter, I'll describe how I helped Peggy and Steve appreciate and harness Rocky's natural skills so he could effectively learn to follow their lead and respect their need to have a trustworthy, well-adjusted dog. Rocky, like the majority of my dog clients, had only been exposed to conventional training in sterile, indoor settings—and he'd flunked out many times over. But when he went through my out-of-the-box basic training program that fuses dogs' smarts and abilities with their need for human pack leadership, exercise, mental stimulation and novel environments, all parties were able to cultivate mutual respect and share in the success of a healthy, happy interspecies bond.

Treats might hypnotize a dog into obeying once in a while, but in that case, they aren't listening to the trainer or the owner; they're listening to the treat. This situation sets everyone up for failure, and the dog pays the ultimate price. Most of the dogs I see euthanized every single month were treat trained. Yet, for some reason, this method of so-called training has become known as "positive reinforcement." If this is positive training, then why is the ultimate result so often death?

If you look closely at what's happening at those yearly supermodel dog fashion-show events, you'll notice that the dogs are always staring at the treat pouch, not the person. It's the dirtiest trick of the trade. So many trainers use treats. They'll often tell you not to feed your dog before you head to training class so the dog has no choice but to obey during the training class. But in the real world, the bait is rarely ever as satisfying as what your pooch might find on even a square foot of sidewalk. By comparison, a bird, a squirrel or anything else that moves looks far more delicious than a silly little treat.

Imagine yourself walking down the street with your treat-trained dog, your pocket stuffed full of goodies. Your pet graduated from some six-week course in a sterile training centre, where he picked up some basic commands like sit, stay, heel and come, for which he was always rewarded with food.

You're feeling pretty confident because a professional trained your dog. Then all of a sudden, a squirrel or a cyclist or a woman pushing her baby in a stroller appears across the street. Your dog bolts, the leash slips out of your hand and a second later, a car hits your dog. Or he manages to get across the street and starts chasing after the squirrel, cyclist or woman with the baby stroller. You run after the dog, yelling, "Stop!" but he knows you have nothing to offer him but a treat. He's not hungry, and the treat can't compete with the thrill of the chase. What's the treat worth now? Diddlysquat. You can yell your face off with verbal commands, but that dog is not going to listen.

And now you're facing another potentially deadly situation. Dogs typically attack from the rear, and once they get into predatory chase mode, who knows what's going to happen? Maybe he'll run twenty blocks after that squirrel, become lost and end up at a shelter. Maybe he won't attack anyone this time, but if you do eventually catch up to him and find him snarling at the terrified woman and her screaming baby, and if you slip him a treat to try to calm him down, you may as well have said, "Good boy. Nice job protecting me against this sinister baby." You're enforcing dangerous behaviour, and one of these days it's going to bite you in the proverbial butt—and hurt an innocent bystander or your dog or both.

Even mellow dogs who would otherwise show no signs of aggression can act out around treats. You know how kids' snacks tend to collect in the seat of a baby stroller? Well, I once saw a dog at a park beeline for a stroller-bound kid. He licked the kid's hand, then immediately started Hoovering around the seat, snuffling like a pig searching for truffles *while the kid was still in the stroller.* Within two seconds he'd pushed the entire stroller over onto the grass, trying to get at that booty. Luckily, the kid wasn't hurt, but what if that had happened on a sidewalk?

There's nothing sweet or gentle about treat training, yet for some strange reason, my antitreat stance has earned me a rogue, badass reputation in the industry. But if it means preventing more dogs from becoming crack-headed monsters, I'll consider the less-than-complimentary labels badges of honour.

People need to understand that they're being taken for a very dangerous, not to mention expensive, ride when they sign up with treat trainers. These courses result in an empty wallet and a false sense of security that can easily snowball into chaos and, ultimately, heartache. They contribute to many negative behaviours: dogs saddled with the alpha role, which is the primary cause of every single conceivable negative issue, including jumping up, horrifying table manners and territorial aggression that can lead to deadly bites.

The simple fact that dogs *develop* even more serious negative behaviour problems once they receive treat training should make it more than obvious that treat training doesn't work. But people will often think, "Well the pros say it's correct. Must be something wrong with my dog." They bark at their dogs for acting up, yet the treats keep on coming. What does that say to the dog? It says, "Looky here, I've got a chump for a boss. I can do whatever I want and Two Legs will slip me a reward no matter what." What a tragic, vicious circle! Now the dog's addicted to bad behaviours, and we humans literally feed the frenzy, acting more and more like strung-out drug pushers.

As I've said before, let's not forget that dogs have forty-two teeth just like wolves and foxes. A dog is not a child with four legs; it's an *animal*. The treat trainers refuse to acknowledge this simple fact, so it's your job to stand up for your dog. If the so-called method of training doesn't make sense, question the teacher, not your dog.

The Ugly Side of Beauty Pageants

My first exposure to treat trainers happened way back in the late eighties, when I went behind the scenes at a dog show. What I saw there had a profound effect on my life and a huge impact on my philosophies about dog training.

I couldn't believe all the primping these supermodel dogs had to go through: the hairsprays, the hair dyes and colouring, the hair dryers and the teams of stylists brandishing brushes and grooming tools, slaving away on each dog to get things "just right." (When I saw the beagle that won last year in the all-breed category, I loved it. There may have been some colour enhancing, but no one could have trimmed and styled that coat.)

I didn't know about the dangers of treats at that point. I didn't even know that treats were used to teach dogs at all, but then nothing in that place made sense to me. I approached three different women to ask them about their training methods. Every single one of them said that dogs are stupid and can only be trained to follow a few rudimentary commands—and only if they're bribed with treats. Naturally, this sentiment made me really mad. I knew it wasn't true, and it was extra ridiculous coming from people blow-drying and styling dogs' hair.

To be fair, I have met maybe a dozen incredible breeders and individuals in the dog show world who actually strive to educate and expose their dogs to many environments besides the ring. But one thing I learned that day is that if you want a dog to function in the real world, you need to find methods that actually teach them to become good dog citizens, harnessing their smarts and dog needs instead of their fickle bellies.

Dog Bait: Fool's Gold

Back here in the real world, many of my clients have been duped by treat trainers. Some have firsthand experience of the negative impact treats have on their dog, and they're looking for a better way. They've gone to prospective trainers and said, "I don't want to use treats," and far too often, the so-called experts have responded with, "Then we won't train your dog and you'll never have success." Blah, blah, blah. One of my clients saw twelve trainers in ten months. They all tried to sell her the same line, and they were downright hostile when she challenged their thinking. I applaud my clients for sticking to their guns, but it makes me sick that there are so many trainers out there pushing this crap, disrespecting dogs and people and ruining so many lives.

If you've been conned into dealing with these characters and you've already paid your money, I encourage you to challenge the trainer. Say, "Show me how to do this without using bribes." Request that the trainer work with your dog outside sterile, indoor training environments and see if he can actually teach your dog to follow even the most basic command, with or without treats. I'm not a betting man, but I'd be willing to bet cold, hard cash that the trainer will fail. I've already challenged one animal behaviourist, but he continues to refuse to believe that treat training is bad for dogs, and he keeps on pushing his zombie dog beliefs on the world.

Doggy Rehab

Some of my clients are harder to talk out of the treat addiction than others at first. They're addicted, too, and they're utterly afraid of going through the withdrawal process, which I admit can get ugly. When treats are yanked, some dogs will manipulate their owners by saying, "Well, in that case, I'm not going to eat at all." Two days later, the owner feels badly and caves. That means everyone's back at square one before that dog has even finished snorting up her first post-manipulation treat. That's a crafty, addict dog at work. So instead of giving in, you have to ride out the hunger strike. A dog is going to eat eventually—within four days, to be exact. In the meantime, the dog will use all sorts of manipulation in hopes that you'll give up on training. He'll beg and beg, and if you cave, whether it's a week later or a month later, your dog will be back in the driver's seat, steering you once again toward doom. Here, once again, consistency is key, especially when you're trying to undo the damage perpetrated by treat training.

One dog I worked with refused her owner's food as soon as her training treats were yanked. But when I put some healthy food in front of her, she ate immediately. The owner tried again: refusal. Finally, she started crying and said, "It's breaking my heart." "Well, it should," I replied. "Your dog is kicking your ass." When she realized that the dog was taking advantage of her, she was furious. She felt used, violated. Eventually, after we'd worked hard to teach her dog to become a great dog citizen, she came to appreciate that her dog's craftiness was a sign of intelligence. She was able to laugh about it, and today it's a running joke at her dinner parties, which are much more pleasant now that her dog has excellent manners.

Dogs will do all sorts of things to manipulate their owners, but treat trainers haven't given these animals any better choices. At the very least, consider all the money you'd have to spend every year for likely sixteen years or more on this doggy crack. Consider that could buy you a home, an education for your kids, vacations and a life—with a stable dog companion along for the ride instead of a monster.

Get rid of whatever the dog is addicted to and see what his true colours are. How can there be so much power in a tiny little piece of kibble, a morsel of beef? How did we come to this place?

BAITING AND DYSFUNCTIONAL DOG ATTENTION

Dogs are more likely to obey their owners' commands without food bait, according to a study by researchers at the Vienna-based Clever Dog Lab.[23] They studied the obedience levels of sixteen dogs while their owners looked at their dogs, read, watched TV, turned their backs and left the room altogether.[24] The studies were done in the dogs' own homes, providing a much more intimate setting than that of a sterile lab. The researchers used food baits in one of three experiments.

Dog owners commanded their dogs to lie down on the ground, and they were timed to follow that command for up to sixty seconds. In all of the experiments, dogs sustained greater attention when their owners were looking at them, showing that pooches are more likely to obey when their owners are focused on them.

But when food was involved, dogs remained lying down for much shorter periods of time, no matter what their owners were doing. During the non-food experiments, the canines averaged forty-five to fifty-five seconds, compared to fifteen to forty-five seconds when food was around. They also continued to obey the lie-down command in almost 80 per cent of all situations, compared to 50 per cent in the experiments where food bait was used. Without food bait, the periods of time that the dogs continued to sit ranged from thirty-five to sixty seconds. With food, dogs sometimes stood up within seconds, even when their owners were looking directly at them.

When owners left the room altogether (leaving some non-bait food in the room that could tempt the dogs), dogs continued lying down for an average of forty-five seconds, compared to fifteen seconds in the food bait experiments. And ten of the sixteen dogs in the food experiments broke the lie-down command and chowed down the food left in the room to tempt them.

Dog-Training Fads: The Negative Implications of "Positive Reinforcement" Techniques

Treat training became popular in the 1980s as a "positive" method of dog training, and pretty soon, virtually everyone and their dogs were totally hooked on it. In my opinion, this sort of so-called humane training was something like the rebound effect people experience after divorce: because the relationship turned toxic, you look for a new partner who's the complete opposite of the old one. Most of the time, the rebound partner is merely a speed bump on the road to finding a healthy new relationship.

Treat training was a reaction to old-school, aggressive, boot camp–style training methods—the type of training that involved physically bullying, scaring and embarrassing dogs into submission and obedience. Some old-school trainers believed that dogs, by nature, are stupid creatures. Well, "Stupid is as stupid does," and that's no way to train a dog, let alone establish and nurture a healthy bond. So most people in the industry agreed that better, more respectful training methods needed to be found. I personally wouldn't even have sampled treat training en route to finding a better way because I believed (and still believe) that dog trainers should help people and their dogs *learn*. But I guess some trainers and animal behaviourists were desperate to come up with *something* they believed might serve as an alternative to the status quo.

People make mistakes—that's a given. You can't always hit your stride without first falling on your face. But, unfortunately, two decades later, treat training isn't seen as a curious sidebar in the history of dog training. It has actually *gained* popularity.

If treat training is truly effective and respectful of an individual's intelligence, why isn't it used in human schools? Why not have a whole new school system in which parents are ordered not to feed their kids breakfast and where there's a vending machine in every classroom, doling out candy bars for good marks and positive behaviour? Would you enroll your kid in that kind of "school"? Of course not. So why sign your dog up for a program like that?

Ironically, the old-school, negative methods of training are still also around today, with many trainers recommending prong, choke and electric collars. Some will also use ridiculous stunts meant to humiliate dogs. For example, one of these "specialists" throws a blanket over a dog's head, and if the dog doesn't immediately shake the blanket off, she's labelled "stupid." What if your dog was subjected to training like that and he just happened to be too tired to drop the blanket on the floor? What if he was claustrophobic or lacked confidence—or was so mellow that nothing bothered him? Doesn't that stunt sound like the school dunce-cap method? Oh, yeah, that worked like a charm too.

One of my clients asked a treat trainer to show her how to get her dog to sit and stay without treats. The trainer tried using verbal commands, and when that didn't work, the trainer said, "Well, your dog's just not smart." The trainer didn't show her how to establish alpha status and learn to bond and communicate effectively or even to use other command methods, like snapping or hand signals. When I met that dog and tried finger snapping, he was doing sit-stay consistently within three minutes and forty-five seconds. The dog wasn't stupid and neither was his owner. As soon as these partners had a few alternative tools for success, they were on the road to realizing their full potential.

Red Flags for Food-Related Aggression

Dogs who've developed food-related aggression can become very dangerous whenever they're around food and other people or dogs. When a dog with this type of behaviour is brought to me, I have to assess many factors before under-standing whether or not she actually has become dangerous. Here's a list of some signals that indicate that you need to take those aggressive behaviours very seriously and use extreme caution with your dog when she's around food, whether it's her own dish, a bone or any human food:

* Your dog gives a very deep, low growl or bares his teeth when anyone is around his bowl—or even when someone enters the kitchen or any other space where he eats.
* Your dog nips at people and other dogs or has snatched human food from human hands.
* Your dog exhibits any aggressive behaviour when other dogs or people are around her dog food, her dog bones or human food.

If your dog shows any of these signs of food-related aggres-sion, it is imperative that you at least keep other people, especially children, away from your dog while she's eating. Once this behavioural issue has become entrenched, the dog really has no control over herself around food, whether it's her own meal or any human food. So it's your responsibil-ity to make sure that no one is harmed around your dog and that your dog is safeguarded from harming others. Even with good professional guidance, some of these dogs can never become comfortable when they're around food and other people or dogs. They might have absolutely no other aggressive behaviours, but you'll need to be extra-vigilant and respectful of their food-related anxieties. If your dog is like this, give her a wide berth around her food bowl and keep people and other dogs away from her while she's eating.

Instruct other family members to steer clear of her dish and her chew bones and never let anyone try to feed her any food, especially treats, by hand.

The best ways to prevent this potentially deadly behaviour are as follows: do not do treat training with your dog, never let your dog eat human food and train your dog to relinquish control of anything and everything that he might put in his mouth. (See Chapters 6 and 9 for tug games and other methods that teach dogs to respect the hands that feed them.) If your dog is already exhibiting these aggressive behaviours, don't try to attempt any hands-on behavioural training yourself. But be very careful to choose a professional who really knows how to handle aggressive dogs. It's a buyer-beware world out there.

FOOD-RELATED AGGRESSIONS

*A*ccording to research done at the Department of Clinical Veterinary Medicine at the University of Cambridge,[25] children are most commonly bitten by dogs when the canines are in "food-guarding" mode. Forty-two per cent of incidents involve children the dog knew and 53 per cent involve kids the dog was not familiar with. Nineteen per cent of the biting dogs in this study had never bitten a human before, and 66 per cent had attended "obedience training" classes.

Out-of-the-Box Training

Some people call my dog-training methods unconventional and even weird. But would you take a surfing lesson from someone that couldn't surf? Let's say you did decide to take training like that. In a room in some warehouse, the instructor will show you all the introductory basics, such as how to position yourself on the board, how to paddle and how to pop up to the standing position. Then, as soon as it's time to head out to the beach, he splits, leaving you to fend for yourself in the waves thundering toward the shore.

Shouldn't a dog trainer be able to guide you into the "waves" of dog behaviour and help you learn how to ride them? I think it's weird—and dangerous—to train people and their dogs in a sterile box. With both private and group training, I introduce my clients to a variety of different environments and situations: unfamiliar dog parks, busy city streets, hotels and office towers with revolving doors, elevators and narrow stairwells and transit systems that allow dogs, like Calgary's commuter trains. The goal is to understand the strengths and limitations of both species. Typically, dogs adapt impressively to all sorts of scenarios—it's the people who often pack their own fears, phobias and insecurities and bring them along for the ride.

I meet many of my clients after they've gone through a string of trainers. The training attempts have failed, and they still have an unruly dog on their hands, so the failure has got under their own skin. They don't trust their dogs and they don't trust themselves, and this often causes them to give up on training and even isolate their dogs. I'm not brought in to fix people, but nine times out of ten, human confidence levels in these situations are at an all-time low. This just makes human-dog relations even more stressful and difficult to mend. And it can destroy the self-esteem of even the most successful and confident people.

Rocky's Road

By the time I met Rocky (the Australian shepherd), he'd been to so many dud trainers that it was really tough to get him on-board with training. He seemed to have lost faith that any human could actually teach him anything. The first time I met him and asked him to sit, he looked sideways at me as if to say, "Oh, no, here we go again. Another bonehead." I immediately knew I'd have to bring in a huge mix of settings and activities to maintain Rocky's interest, and as it turned out, the training program I developed for him was the most extensive one I ever created.

As I mentioned earlier, Steve and Peggy acquired Rocky because they really wanted more balance in their lives. They had accomplished so many great things professionally and wanted a great home life as well. "We were both first-time dog owners and we really had no clue about dog behaviours," admits Steve. "And for the first four years, Rocky really just added more stress to our lives. He was the king of the castle and had no respect for us. We didn't realize it at the time, but we'd been spoiling Rocky in all the wrong ways—by giving him alpha status, letting him sleep with us (with his head on the pillow) and rewarding him for bad behaviours with treats. Our vet would joke that Rocky was a "furry person," but the behavioural problems kept escalating. When we went outside, we never knew for sure what was going to happen. Rocky was probably picking up on our stress and taking advantage of his alpha status, chasing every squirrel in the neighbourhood."

Steve and Peggy had worked with five trainers over that four-year stretch; four trainers used treats and another was physically abusive. None provided this family with the knowledge or tools they needed to assert their human alpha status, much less harness Rocky's great skills, smarts and abilities. As time went by, the balance of power just kept tipping more and more toward Rocky, causing a vicious circle of issues. "Rocky would lunge at anything on wheels: skateboarders, cyclists and rollerbladers," says Peggy. "After a while he started grabbing my jacket cuffs and would swirl me around in circles. Once, a friend and I took him for a walk in the park and he literally started running circles around us, lunging and trying to nip. It was downright scary."

"Then we met Brad and thought, 'Well, it's worth a shot,'" pipes in Steve. "Other than putting Rocky down or trying to find a farm that would take him, we couldn't conceive of any other out."

For me it was just another "last-resort" case, but luckily, the dog and humans involved were very serious, hardworking individuals who were ready, willing and able to step up to the plate.

"We knew enough to understand that Rocky wasn't failing us; we were letting Rocky down," says Steve. "It causes a lot of guilt and stress. Our confidence was really low when we met Brad, which made his out-of-the-box training methods seem even more challenging: 'You want us to take *this* dog downtown? to a cattle ranch?' It sounded crazy at first, but we decided to suspend judgment and try it out. It was kind of like training in the military. But when you go through the process, you prove to yourself that you can do it. You realize quickly that a key goal is to not just train the dog; it's to build up people's confidence so that the dog respects you. It's very interesting the way simple tasks like umbilical training, no talking and running around at the dog park develop your leadership skills. Especially for people who aren't very athletic, like Peggy."

"Training was a hardcore experience," admits Peggy. "Brad took us way out of our comfort zones. We had to take Rocky out on busy streets with rush-hour traffic and off-leash, which had been unthinkable to us. But it was critical for Rocky to trust us and know that we were in command. We realized that Rocky had really just been frustrated that we weren't taking charge."

As soon as I started working with Rocky, I realized there was a brilliant, amazing dog lurking beneath the surface, yearning to learn skills. Dogs don't like to be out of control and agitated 24/7 any more than humans do, but Rocky had been given no tools to help him cool his heels and obey the rules. He was actually craving to be educated, but that education needed to be crystal clear and it needed to constantly challenge his smarts and skills.

It makes me so angry to think that if Rocky hadn't had such dedicated parents, he might have been hit by a car, dumped at a shelter or, worse, euthanized for hurting another dog or a human. Rocky is a unique and special dog, and with time and effort, his true brilliance was finally able to shine through. All dogs and all dog parents deserve a crack at that. It starts with acknowledging that treat bribes and other props, like choke and prong collars, aren't effective or positive training tools. Most of the time, dog owners know this already; they just need to learn the tools that will actually bring them success.

I'm not saying that my training methods are always easy.

Sometimes it's like kicking the crutches away from someone who doesn't even know how to walk, much less run. So there might be plenty of stumbling at first. There might be tears of frustration. There might even be setbacks for both the people and the dogs. But wouldn't you rather chase success than spend likely at least sixteen years chasing after your dog, never being able to catch up?

GOOD VERSUS BAD DOG GENES?

*R*esearchers at the Family Dog Project in Budapest have conducted a wide range of fascinating problem-solving experiments with dogs and have found no scientific correlations between any breed and the behaviours of dogs within that group. The researchers also note that personal characteristics ranging from fearfulness to confidence varied considerably among breeds and that "The only breed-specific differences we found were that the owner of mixed-breed dogs showed poorer anthropomorphic [humanizing] attitudes toward their pets."[26] In other words, humans set the tone for their dogs' abilities by influencing dogs' individual experiences and social environments.

University of Florida researchers believe that breed-profiling methods "lead not only to a misguided fear of well-behaved dogs identified with a 'bad' breed, but may also offer a false sense of security around a dog showing warning signs of aggression just because it comes from a breed with a good reputation." Instead, they say, "The type of owner, not the breed of the dog, is the best predictor for dog attacks." [27]

Street Safety Training: Sit, Stay, Come and Stop

Training Rocky to respect and follow basic commands was a critical aspect of our training program. It's the backbone of all dog training because it teaches our dogs to follow our commands consistently and safeguards them against harm. It also sets the stage for training off-leash so dogs can safely enjoy independence and freedom. Some of my clients downplay the importance of this basic training because they have the idea that it's unnecessary and even demeaning to their dog's intelligence. But dogs like to learn and show off their skills. Basic training allows them to do this, and it's also a great way to keep them engaged and stimulated.

Most dogs take to my sit-stay training methods with a lot of enthusiasm, and many find the process quite easy—but not Rocky! He'd attended, and flunked out of, so many conventional training programs, that the process was much more difficult for him. Rocky had become so defiant that it was really tough trying to get him to do anything. He just wanted to run around. Rocky was so used to controlling everything that happened around him that when I first tried to gain his attention, he'd just shrug me off. I always incorporate training into everyday life activities, and with Rocky, it was mandatory to provide a variety of different settings. Even getting a bit of daily micro-training in with Rocky was tough. You couldn't even say, "Rocky, come." Rocky just wasn't going to come, and every failed attempt scored him another win. So I slipped the training into everything, the way you slip veggies into kids' food.

Teaching Sit

I recommend doing this initial training using non-verbal commands, so you can start this training during the umbilical, no talking period. After that, you can begin attaching verbal commands to your chosen gestures and signals, but avoid repetition so the command counts. If your dog doesn't respond to the mix of verbal and non-verbal, go back to the non-verbal until she learns to associate one with the other.

Many dogs take to the sit command easily. Often, a dog will sit if you stand directly in front of him, with your body square to the dog. As I said in the previous chapter, I don't think verbal commands should be used during initial training because dogs respond much better to movement and gestures like these.

Leash-Guided Sit Method

If your dog doesn't sit in response to other non-verbal commands, such as a snap or any hand gesture you might use, don't push her backside and hind legs down with your hands because that can cause serious nerve damage and lead to hip problems. The leash-guided method is a much more effective physical way to guide the dog into sitting position. Here's how to do it:

* Hold onto the leash about eight to ten inches (twenty to twenty-five centimetres) from the dog's collar clasp.
* Pull up on the leash so the dog's neck and head tilt upward and his butt tilts downward, to the ground, like a teeter-totter.
* For Rocky, we had to go a bit further and pull the leash upward until his paws were floating off the ground, so his body tipped slightly backward and he would sit instinctively.

"I don't believe in any form of physical discipline, so I was uncomfortable using the leash to control Rocky," admits

Peggy. "But it was apparent that Brad's leash methods didn't harm Rocky physically. He's such a strategic thinker, so if they had, he would probably have manipulated us into quitting the program. It helped that Max and Dez were there much of the time to show how dogs discipline other dogs."

Some dogs will react to any request to sit, physical or not, by engaging in overly dramatic submissive behaviour. Drama queens! They exhibit all kinds of wonderful talents in master manipulation, like dropping down flat to the ground, yelping, screeching, dropping their ears, rolling on their bellies right away or twirling around. These are clear signs of a manipulative alpha dog who's trying to control the situation, and that means the owner probably has a record of submitting to the pooch.

With dogs who act this way, you have to persist in getting them to sit instead of going into one of these submissive positions. I've seen some pretty serious dog disciplines and I've never seen dogs engage in exaggerated movements when they're in pain. Don't cave! Interrupt the drama-queen behaviour by making that dog sit. It might take eight attempts or twenty-eight, but redirect the movement into something you want, not what the dog wants.

With dogs that haven't developed behaviour issues, the next step is relatively easy:

* After the dog has been sitting for at least thirty seconds, start walking around for a while, making sure to lead, and refrain from touching the leash itself, letting the leash drag on the ground.
* Stop and face the dog again. Some dogs will sit right away. Other dogs might need a command like a snap or a hand gesture, which you can do in combination with the leash-guided sit method that I outlined above.

* This time, get the dog to sit for fifteen seconds.
* Move around again and repeat the sit, this time for twenty seconds.
* After the first three successful sits, give your dog some praise with a nice chest scrunch. (As mentioned in Chapter 2, here's how you do a chest scrunch: with your fingertips, massage your dog's chest for a few seconds, in the area between the top of her legs.)
* Notch up the sit duration until your dog can sit for three to five minutes, but keep going back and forth between shorter and longer durations, so your dog doesn't get bored. (Consistency and repetition are keys to training, but don't get caught up in too much linear thinking.) The number of times you repeat the process depends on the individual dog. Some dogs need a lot of repetition. Others need to strengthen their ability to focus, in which case more play breaks or shorter sessions are necessary. Dogs that haven't been given enough daily exercise will naturally also be more distracted during training because they'd rather go for a romp at the dog park when you get home from work. In that case, do some sessions at the park and start your training session with some exercise. Once you get into the exercises, watch out for any signs that your dog is losing interest or is tired or frustrated. If that happens, repeat the amount of time she last sat successfully so you can wrap on a win.

The next step is to teach the dog to sit at intersections. To safeguard your dog, there should be about a six-foot (about two-metre) buffer zone, or more, between the dog and the curb. The exact distance will depend on the length of your dog from snout to tail combined with the length of your leash. Once your dog is able to sit consistently by your side near the curb, praise her for her efforts and move on to the stay training steps described below.

Rocky was such a smart dog that I suspect if he'd been adequately trained from the beginning, he would have mastered these basics really quickly. But he'd become so set in his ways and so suspicious of people that it took weeks to build up his trust. In one sit training session, we might get only ten paces along the hallway heading toward the front door. I would get Rocky to walk a couple of paces toward the door and then get him to sit. Then we'd walk a few more paces and he'd sit. The problem was that each time, after a couple of seconds of sitting, he would raise his butt and we'd have to start all over again. At first he lost interest so quickly that dragging out a session would just have irritated all of us. We knew he was fatigued or frustrated when his body language slowed down. During the initial weeks, his eyes would sometimes turn bloodshot after fifteen minutes—that's how much of an alpha power struggle Rocky put out over even the simplest task.

During the next sit session, we might get down the front pathway. During the third micro-unit, we'd do a bit of weaving around trees to keep Rocky stimulated by switching things up and highlighting his great coordination skills.

Teaching Stay

If you live in a house, start this training at your front door. If you're in an apartment with narrow corridors, find a park where you can tie the leash to a tree, bench or bike rack. The front door is ideal—you'll see why in a minute. Here's how to do it:

* Tie the leash to the inside knob of the front door (with the front door closed).
* Get your dog to sit by the closed door.
* Make a stop motion by throwing your hand out, palm facing the dog, to indicate, "Stay" or "Wait."

* Get your dog to stay sitting for thirty seconds. If she attempts to break the stay at all, consider keeping your hand poised in the stop motion for the duration of the exercise.
* Reward her with a chest scrunch.
* Build up to a minute of sitting, followed by another chest scrunch.

* Now open the front door, with the dog still sitting inside while you go outside and down the front walk.
* Try to get your dog to sit for two minutes. If she tries to get up and follow you, the door will close behind her, so her movement will be restricted by the leash and she shouldn't be able to bolt. If the dog does break from the stay, place her back where she started, close the front door and go through the process again.

Keep practising this exercise whenever you can and in a variety of settings until your dog can stay for up to twenty minutes.

Teaching Come

You can practise this one indoors or in an enclosed outdoor space like a backyard or tennis court.

* Get the dog to sit for about a minute.
* Back up about three steps, get down on your haunches and open your arms wide the way you'd do to encourage a toddler to walk toward you. I don't recommend using verbal commands during the initial training period, but after two weeks, you can start adding, "Come" or "Hustle" in an enthusiastic, medium-pitch tone.
* When your dog runs to you, give him a good chest scrunch.
* Repeat this exercise, getting the dog to sit for different lengths of time, from thirty seconds up to a few minutes, and then come to you.
* Gradually increase your distance until you're about twenty steps away from your dog.

* Acclimatize your dog to responding to "Come" and "Hustle" in a variety of scenarios: whenever you're ready to leave the house with your dog, on your driveway after a car outing, at the park, to wrap up a fetch session in the backyard. But never use this exercise to say goodbye because you'll tease your dog into thinking she's about to get some bonding time and she'll feel burned if that's not the case. This will discourage her and make the command less effective.

Teaching Stop

Now your dog is ready to learn how to stop on command. This is definitely the most important verbal command for your dog to learn—it could save your dog's life. Now you have a free ticket to unzip it so that in times of imminent danger, you'll be able to safeguard your dog quickly. Again, remember to use confident body language and a calm, but firm tone.

* Place your dog in a sit-stay.
* Stand about two feet (a bit more than half a metre) in front of him.
* Gradually back up, facing your dog and increasing your distance to four feet (a bit more than one metre).
* Call your dog to come, but as soon as he starts moving, say, "Stop" while at the same time putting your hand, palm forward, in front of you at the level of your dog's head. The action should be done

quickly. If you've judged the distance spot-on, the dog's head should touch your palm or be within millimetres of your palm.

* Repeat this exercise and then move back in one-foot (about thirty-centimetre) increments. Increase the distance only if your dog put on the breaks as soon as he heard your command. Allow no creeping of one or two paces. It could make the difference between life and death.

* If your dog doesn't stop on that first command, don't continue yelling, "Stop, stop, stop!" In an off-leash setting, your dog might end up being struck by a car if you do that. As I said earlier, the more we repeat any command or correction, the more desensitized the dog becomes. So make that first "Stop" command count, and if your dog breaks out of a stop, place him back in his most recent stay spot.

Basics Graduation Party

At this point your dog has earned many stripes and is ready to begin gearing up for the ultimate reward: off-leash training, which I'll describe in the next chapter. It took months to guide Rocky to this point in training. But after that, he got the freedom he'd been craving all along, and now he is a regular off-leash dog. "We can take Rocky off-leash all the time," says Peggy. "He still likes to take charge sometimes, but we've learned how to play stimulating games that keep us in the driver's seat but that also keep him engaged. Now we have a much closer relationship with Rocky."

Rocky is now one of my helper dogs and an awesome companion. I call on him to teach other dogs the rules of conduct. "The process took about a year," adds Steve. "It wasn't easy, but it was worth every minute. Now we have leadership and can enjoy Rocky for the reasons we wanted a dog in the first place: to remind us there's more to life than work. Now that we enjoy each other's company, we can get out in the fresh air, which is a great stress buster and also keeps us engaged in our community. Rocky helps keep us grounded. Now all of our lives are much more laid back."

Two Types of Learners

All dogs learn in one of two different ways: either instinctively or through repetition. Your dog's learning style will have nothing to do with her breed; instead, it's about her unique personality. I once worked with three dogs from the same litter, all completely different: one was wired for sound and easily distracted and therefore needed a lot of repetition; another was very regal and prim and a stickler for following the rules; and the third was a teacher's pet, hanging on every move and saying, "Okay, got it. What's next?" What kind of dog is yours? Tap into your dog's personality and don't get stuck in a breed rut. Some Border collies might herd geese right away, even as puppies. Other Border collies need to be shown the ropes again and again, and they might never want to herd. A golden retriever might learn to sit in four days—or four months. Dogs who've been removed from their litter before nine weeks of age have been denied critical schooling from their dog mom and dog siblings. As I'll discuss in more detail in Chapters 7 and 9, these animals can have a tough time learning the rules of conduct. If owners aren't given this information, it's no wonder some of them become frustrated quickly and get rid of the dog.

If your dog is a repetitious learner and needs to be instructed over and over again, please understand that he needs a great deal of patience from you, as well as effort, time, consistency and dedication. The training *will* eventually result in success—as long as you're consistent with it and willing to dedicate time and energy to teaching your dog. Rocky was actually an instinctual learner, but for the first six months, he was so entrenched in his household alpha status that it took a lot of time for him to start opening up to the idea that any Two Legs could teach him anything useful.

Many dogs take quite naturally to following simple verbal commands or learning through other methods like finger snapping and hand signals. But I implore you to test your dog's skills in a variety of environments—at the dog park and on the streets, for instance—where there are many different types of stimuli that could distract her and lead to life-threatening accidents. Does your dog always follow your commands when you're in places like these? Brilliant. But if your dog bolted after a rollerblader before you could get her to sit patiently for a minute, I hope you'll consider trying my training methods. As I discuss in Chapter 10, your dog might have hit an age when she needs a refresher course.

Doggy Discipline

As I've mentioned before, a dog will physically discipline another dog when he's breaking the rules of engagement. This will rarely result in injury, but a swift peck or nip will be used to discipline bad behaviour. Is a dog's mother acting abusively or with cruel intentions when she shows her pup the rules and boundaries? Absolutely not. She is simply and beautifully showing him the ropes, with his best interests in mind. I told you about Dez showing me how dogs discipline dogs. Hartley, one of my clients, witnessed a similar situation when he took Spencer, his golden retriever to visit his doggy mom at the breeder. Spencer was five months old at the time and wildly rambunctious. (It was about a year later that I met the family to start working on training.) "We set out on a walk with Spencer's mom," says Hartley. "Spencer was even more excited than usual and he started jumping up at her face. She snarled at him, but he didn't stop. So the next time he came at her, she literally plucked him out of the air by the neck and pinned him to the ground for about ten seconds. It was like she was saying, 'Look, I brought you into this world and if you don't behave, I'll take you out.'"

Remember, though, that when you use physical actions to manage your dog, never use a lot of muscle. It's not about strength; it's about the speed of action and the element of surprise.

By using physical gestures effectively, but never abusively, you will be doing your best to protect your dog from physically harming herself and/or others. In fact, by neglecting to discipline bad behaviour, the dog will be confused, stressed out and ill equipped to conform to any social rules, which could have disastrous and deadly consequences for humans and for dogs. Does a police officer pay you money or pat you on the head for running a red light? for breaking the law in other ways? Of course not. Discipline and praise need to be balanced and consistent, conforming to both human standards *and* the doggy rules of conduct.

My disciplinary methods are much less physically aggressive than those used among dogs. I also don't use old-school intimidation and humiliation methods, and I don't disrespect the intelligence of dogs by leaning on useless props. But like a mother dog's way, my methods are designed so that dogs can *learn* how to behave.

Remember that the secret ingredients for any successful interruption and correction are speed and timing. A dog can move her mouth seven times faster than the human hand, so you have to make sure to move your body really fast. And if you don't discipline immediately, or at least as soon as you discover that a rule has been broken, you will actually be reinforcing bad behaviours.

Successful Interruption and Correction Methods

To maintain the element of surprise, it's best to mix up corrections—particularly with mature dogs who develop behavioural issues later in life. You may have to try different interruptions and corrections before you find the ones that work best for your dog's personality. And the type of discipline you use will also depend on the severity of the crime.

Interruptions can be as simple as a firm verbal command like "Hustle" if you want to get your dog to come to you at the dog park or "Leave it" if you hear your dog click-clicking over to the garbage can. The key is to use verbal commands sparingly so your dog doesn't get into the habit of tuning you out.

Other interruptions are physical, but they're fake-outs— like when a basketball player flops down on the ground hoping the referee will blow the whistle on his opponent so he can get a crack at a couple of free throws. Of course, the situation is different with training a dog. You're not faking an action in order to cheat. You're imitating a mother dog's actions, in part, without actually physically touching the dog. You can fake a dog peck by darting your hand down toward the dog's face, neck or shoulder as quickly as possible at a forty-five-degree angle, coming as close to the face as you can without actually touching the dog. This action catches the dog off-guard and delivers a crystal-clear message: "Don't even think about it!"

Here's another technique that's really effective with dogs that jump up at every Tom, Dick or Harriet they meet (or try to jump up at the dinner table): throw your hand down toward the dog's face really fast, with your palm flat and facing downward. Your dog will think, "If I jump up, I'll run into that hand." But remember, this move won't work if you're not fast enough or not consistent with doing this move *every time* the dog attempts to jump up.

The discipline I used most often in dog daycare was "jail" or "timeout." I've seen wolves use a method like this to discipline unruly pack members by drawing them away from the action and isolating them. My version takes that principle and adapts it to dog training by humans. Immediately collar and leash up your dog and tie the leash to a doorknob or banister that's far enough away from the action but still within eyeball range, so the dog knows what he's missing. With really bad behaviours, consider shortening the leash so your dog can't sit or lie down. Leave him in the timeout for at least fifteen minutes and up to forty-five minutes, depending on the severity of the misbehaviour. When the timeout is done, refrain from petting or praising your dog physically or with a gentle or enthusiastic tone of voice. Give your dog the cold shoulder for about twenty minutes afterwards. You might also want to get back on the umbilical for a few days, so you can monitor your dog's behaviour more closely and underline the message that you are in the lead and will take away his freedoms if he misbehaves.

If timeouts don't negate bad behaviours, you might need to get a bit physical. Remember the goal is to mimic the disciplinary actions of dogs but not to be physically abusive in any way.

The most effective physical correction method is a quick leash correction, which I described in Chapter 2. Remember to use a Martingale-style collar that is designed to loosen immediately after you pull on the chain attached to the collar. As I said before, the key isn't brute force; it's speed and concise, firm movement, which gives a clear message that you mean business. Keep your arm close to your side and use your core muscles to direct, not your arm and shoulder. Don't yank at the leash as if you're fighting a large fish at the end of a line and don't tug at the leash over and over and over. The goal is to make one quick, fluid motion to get your dog's attention.

You could also give your dog the equivalent of the kind of hair mush-up that older siblings give their youngers as a sort of "Scram, kiddo" brush-off that doesn't hurt but is downright annoying. At a forty-five-degree angle, slide your hand downward, starting from the area between the dog's ears and going down to just before the dog's snout. Make sure to avoid your dog's nose because the cartilage is fragile. If mushing up your dog's hairdo isn't enough, try an under-the-jaw correction. This one's another favourite with older brothers when they want to put you in your place (but they also know that if they really hurt you, they'll be in big trouble). Again, the movement needs to be quick and done at a 45-degree angle, with your hand cupped, moving sideways and upward to the underside of the jaw. To understand the specific target, pinch the underside of your own chin with your thumb and feel for outer tip of your jawbone.

Remember, these corrections are not about exerting force. The goal is to perform the action quickly enough that you get your dog to look at you and pay attention immediately. Whatever the size of your dog, if he doesn't snap to attention right away, the correction isn't working.

Recap: Effective Dog-Training Techniques

Dogs are smart and creative, and they crave stimulation. It's our job to learn how to cultivate their needs and skills so they can function in a healthy way in our world and trust that we are in control. Here's a checklist of things you can do to develop your own training program—one that maximizes your dog's abilities:

* Introduce your dog to a variety of different places and scenarios. Avoid sterile training environments where your dog can't be easily distracted. That way, you can train your dog to focus effectively in any setting and also provide interesting and novel experiences that keep her stimulated.
* Build up your own confidence levels, so your dog knows you're in command and so she's also aware that you trust her ability to be well behaved.
* Teach your dog how to sit, stay, come and stop. When you teach these skills, you're strengthening your alpha status, danger-proofing your dog and establishing a foundation for off-leash training.
* Wrap up any session when your dog exhibits fatigue

and concentration lapses, but end all training sessions on a win.

* If your dog has negative behaviours, use interruption and correction techniques to prevent him from continuing in that behaviour.

* If your dog commits an offence, use effective, sometimes physical but never abusive disciplinary methods to teach her that the infraction won't be tolerated.

* Remember to be surprised when your dog does something wrong, not when your dog does something right.

CHAPTER FIVE

Six-Legged Health and Fitness

HEALTHY BONDING THROUGH EXERCISE AND SOCIALIZATION

MYTH: A quick walk that fits into your busy schedule is good enough for your dog.

REALITY CHECK: Dogs need a lot of physical and mental stimulation, including time to check out their daily news, socialize with other dogs and (the ultimate doggy reward) enjoy the freedom of going off-leash. By mixing these doggy needs with training sessions, we can foster and strengthen our dogs' skills and make bonding with our dogs a pleasure for both species.

Bisco's Catch-22

Bisco is a party dog. She loves to play with other dogs and romp around. Trouble is, her owners Cathy and Jim have been told you can't take an Irish terrier off-leash. It's true that she liked to play catch-me-if-you-can and often got away on them in the park. So Cathy and Jim never let her off-leash when they took her for walks there. "When other off-leash dogs approached her, she'd yelp and so I'd pull her away," Cathy admits. "She was such a cute puppy, and my instinct was always to rush to her rescue. I'd get so nervous with other off-leash dogs around, running all of these what-if? scenarios in my head."

That doesn't sound like a great time for either species, right? The owners were stressed and fearful that a dog fight might break out, so they white-knuckled the leash whenever other off-leash dogs approached. But those potential doggy friends were exactly the kind of party dogs Bisco wanted to run and frolic and play with. So the excited little puppy would strain on the leash and yelp like a kid dragged from the birthday party before the cake's served—and it happened every day of her young life. Cathy and Jim weren't denying her doggy need for walks, but those walks were so wrought with friction, both literally and figuratively, that Bisco was utterly clueless about how to socialize with other dogs. Every walk in the dog park ended up as a tug-o'-war battle.

That cute puppy had turned into a nightmare dog by the age of four months. "She started to become very dominant and demanding," says Cathy. "The first time she grabbed the end of the toilet paper roll and started running down the hall with it, it was so cute—a Kodak moment—I went running for the camera. But by the third time, I thought I'd lose my mind. Once she almost pushed me down the stairs. Then, one time, Jim was having a bath, and I wouldn't let her in the bathroom. She looked at me defiantly and then peed on my foot. I thought, one of us isn't going to be here in a month. I realized that something had to be done."

My training plan for Bisco included umbilical and agility training to build up the bond of interspecies trust and to teach Bisco to follow her owners' lead, along with a heap of socialization and play with other dogs that fed her need for stimulation. She also got a good dose of outdoor sit-stay training and, once she'd earned her stripes as a well-behaved dog, off-leash training—so the entire family could be active and have fun together.

Exercise is of the utmost importance to dogs. It's also the best way to bond with your dog and develop mutual trust. But far too often, canine companions aren't getting enough exercise, and they're not getting enough variety, including socialization with other dogs and a range of mental stimulation.

I've met so many brilliant and awesome dogs like Bisco who are hungry to run and play, but their owners either neglect those needs or they're too protective and fearful of what might happen as soon as the dog's unleashed. Imagine taking an Olympic sprinter, putting shackles on him and making him stand in the middle of the track and watch people running by? It's no wonder these dogs often develop all sorts of behaviour issues that get worse and worse, causing more tension during dog walks. Sometimes the tensions turns into a battle, and I've noticed that most dog fights occur between a dog that's leashed and another dog that's off-leash.

Dogs need a good, steady mix of physical and mental exercise, but the ultimate reward for any dog is being allowed to go off-leash. I hear far too many people saying things like "Oh beagles can't go off-leash" when they've never even attempted to try off-leash training. If you have low expectations about your dog's individual abilities and potential—you think your dog is too unruly, untrustworthy or incapable or that he's not the right breed—you'll get what *you* expect. But if you offer your dog a variety of experiences, provide good training and have trust in his abilities, he'll prove that he can be off-leash. Let your dog earn that privilege and freedom.

With a little effort, some self-discipline and enthusiasm, you can give your dog all the physical and mental stimulation he needs. You don't have to go hiking in the wilderness for hours every day, but a twenty-minute walk (always around the same block or to the same dog park) won't satisfy your dog. It's better to take him along on your various errands and mix him up in your daily outings than to saddle him with the same routine every day.

Two hours is an ideal amount of time to take your dog for a walk. Many people can't dedicate that much of their day to their dog's exercise, but don't let that be your excuse to neglect your dog's needs altogether. If you're really strapped for time, it's easy to give her some exercise and mental stimulation while you're doing even the most basic chores—whether you're cleaning up the garage or doing the gardening or walking. The key is to keep the dog active by making her part of your daily activities. And you can take your dog practically anywhere these days.

Once you satisfy your dog's basic need for many different types of stimulation, you'll notice that her negative behaviours diminish. And if you've already established the lead household role, those behaviours will almost always disappear completely.

Another benefit of regular exercise is that your dog won't feel as if she has to make the most of any rare opportunity to suck in fresh air and the thousands of other smells that give her the latest news about the 'hood. When a dog who's been starved of outdoor action finally gets some freedom, she'll experience sensory overload and feel anxious or hyper, trying to soak in too much news. She really won't be able to process any of it.

How do you feel after a snowstorm cuts you off from any outside activities or information—No TV, no Internet, no newspapers, little to no socializing, no sunshine and no fresh air? You feel a bit stir-crazy, right? Like your home is a prison. And when the power comes back on and the roads are ploughed, you're keyed up to get outside and drink up all the stimulation you've missed out on. Ditto for a dog who gets little to no taste of the world beyond the window. And ditto for little dogs who are constantly being carried everywhere. By treating them like a lapel decoration, you're literally depriving them of their primary need to sniff out and process the terrain.

DOG WALKING ON THE COAST AND DOWN UNDER

West Coast Canadian dog owners spent almost twice as much time walking than people who didn't own a dog: 300 minutes per week versus 168 minutes.[28] In another survey of Australians, dog walkers averaged 150 minutes weekly, but 23 per cent never walked their dogs.[29]

Quality over Quantity

Once your dog has her fill of exercise and mental stimulation, she'll be able to relax when you go out with friends for an evening or plant yourself on the couch to watch a movie. Recently, we took a trip to Tofino on Vancouver

Island. Rudy and our Rottweiler buddy Jackson came along for the ride. Jackson was wired at the start of the trip, and with every little movement I made, he was up and raring to go. We took the dogs with us exploring and went on quite a challenging hike, over steep, rocky terrain. Jackson slipped a few times, but I was always there to catch him. He probably wouldn't even have tried a sidetrip like that if he wasn't such a confident and well-behaved dog. Same goes for Rudy. He was never saddled with little-dog syndrome and treated like a fragile china doll. Believe me, by the end of the day, those two dogs were contentedly relaxing and snoozing together by the fireplace.

Social Animals

Dogs need to be around their own species, and social structure is as important for them as it is for us. Yet I've met many dogs who have no clue how to socialize. They're socially anxious, fearful or aggressive with other dogs because their social skills have been suppressed. Then, when they finally go to the dog park or meet neighbourhood canines, people wonder why their normally mellow pooch lashes out or rushes at other dogs like a bowling ball looking for a strike. Most of the time, the dog isn't trying to pick a fight, but he's clueless as to how to interact tactfully.

This type of thing also happens in the human world all the time. Say you and I go out to a bar. You see a woman dressed to the nines and you go over to strike up a conversation. She attacks you verbally as if she's fending off a masked avenger in a dark alley. You're not going to stick around and try to draw out some friendlier person who may or may not be lurking underneath. You're going to bolt. A few minutes later, a big dude walks by and clips you with his big shoulder, and you spill your martini. You think, Thanks a lot, dude. But do you immediately go chasing after him, plant yourself in front of his face and start yelling at him? Or do you avoid him? Chances are, you'd avoid him. Maybe the shove was accidental, but whatever the case, you're there to have fun, and kicking up a fuss would be more trouble than it's worth. And if everyone in the club was as obnoxious or careless as these people, nobody would ever go to bars.

Dogs who've never been allowed to grow socially and understand how to let their guard down to say even a simple hello are going to be anxious or downright obnoxious at the dog park. And they'll never know how to act when they're off-leash, which is the doggy equivalent of shaking their butts on the dance floor. Often the behaviour of these dogs makes people withdraw, thinking they have an anti-social pooch on their hands, which just stifles the dog even more. And dog owners can unintentionally stifle their dogs in any number of ways. After a busy week at work, for instance, your idea of a great Friday night might be vegging on the couch, watching a movie. You've already had your fill of human bonding for a while, but if your dog's been homebound all week, she hasn't.

Many of my clients' previous trainers scared them into thinking that their dog was too aggressive to mix with other canines. But nine times out of ten, the first time these clients showed up at group training, their dogs proved not only that they knew how to play nicely, but also that they'd been yearning to mix with other dogs. That set off a chain reaction of positive influences for both species.

It's critical to make sure your dog is socialized with other dogs, ideally at a young age. But it's rarely ever too late to turn your apparently anti-social mutt into a best friend—for other dogs and with you. The key is to put them in a variety of new places that feed the need for variety, instead of the routine rut.

Bisco Busts a Move (and a Common Breed Myth)

After I met Bisco and her owners, I set up a five-point plan: umbilical training to build up the bond of trust and to teach Bisco to respect that her owner was in command; lots of socialization and play with other dogs; agility training to stimulate Bisco's brain and put her mind back in control over her body, not the other way around; outdoor sit-stay training so Bisco would listen to her owners' commands and earn the privilege of going off-leash; and, finally, off-leash training so the entire family could enjoy their park romps.

"The goal was to have higher expectations about Bisco's potential," says Cathy. "I raised children with high expectations, so why did I have such lowered expectations about Bisco? With the outdoor umbilical, every movement was driven by me, and Bisco was always watching me instead of the other way around. I also had to train myself not to fuss and bother when she met other dogs. The group training sessions really helped with that. I saw her getting along with other dogs like Rocky and Dez and Max."

Agility Training

In my one-on-one training, as well as my group "Six Legs to Fitness" workouts, I use agility training to get dogs and humans thinking outside the box, flexing their brain muscles as well as their bodies and socializing with other people and their dogs.

Agility training is like running an obstacle course. It's a great way to train your dog to be attentive and to strengthen his bond of trust in you. And it creates the ideal type of inter-species conversation: providing mental stimulation that also lets your dog build up his coordination and dexterity. This kind of training keeps *you* in shape, too, and fine-tunes your own reflexes so you can move more confidently.

To get started on agility training, you can turn nearly any environment into a dog obstacle course, using walls, stairs, benches, logs, ramps and playgrounds. On days when you're strapped for time, set up a course in your backyard, using any objects you have at hand as pylons that you can navigate around. The goal is to set up a course that allows you to change directions and speed constantly, something like the courses at horse shows but scaled to your dog's height—and yours. Once you have the obstacle course set up, you can start the agility training. Here's how:

* Leash up your dog umbilical style.
* Start walking, jogging or running, depending on both your fitness level and your dog's.
* Make sure you're always dictating the movement and that your dog is following your lead and not pulling on the leash.
* Change your direction, going from side to side and backwards, to really get your dog dialed into moving with you.
* Add obstacles that you can navigate around, such as trees, benches and logs; go up stairs, then come right back down again; use playground equipment, ramps— whatever you have to work with.

You can also take the dog with you while you're doing your favourite forms of exercise and recreation, like blading, biking or running. But don't just make the dog run after you the whole time. Keep her attentive and thinking on her feet by changing your direction periodically or, once your dog can go off-leash, circle back behind her or hide behind a tree and surprise her. And always give your dog some timeouts to converse with other dogs and get whiffs of interesting new smells.

Even on rainy days, you can do all sorts of fun things at home to engage your dog and allow him to use his brain. Put him on umbilical and make some fun out navigating around the furniture—or running up and down the stairs while you're doing chores. You can also play games like hide and seek, which I'll describe in Chapter 6. When the dog finds you, he'll be all jazzed up and enthusiastic because he accomplished something that might seem simple to you but in the dog's view is a very rewarding, work-like activity.

VIBE CHECK

*O*wners of aggressive dogs are much more likely to be "tense," "shy," "emotionally less stable" and "undisciplined" than owners of low-aggression dogs according to research from the Department of Clinical Veterinary Medicine, University of Cambridge.[30]

Human Vibes

My clients who live in fear of dog parks are not horrible people who purposely deny their dogs a decent social life. But after the idea is planted in their heads that their dog can't play nicely with other dogs, it really starts to take root like a weed that spreads, choking the life out of other plants. That's what happened with Cathy and Bisco. From the start of every walk, Bisco yanked at the leash because she was wired for fun at the dog park, and that made Cathy immediately start to tense up. That, in turn, made Bisco think, "Geez, she's anxious today. Better be on high alert." Then as soon as Cathy laid eyes on another dog, particularly an off-leash dog, the anxiety levels increased. That made Bisco think, "Oh, I was right to be on high alert. Better start yapping." And the vicious circle kept spinning around and around, picking up speed.

The Rules of Social Engagement

Parks are a great place to let dogs get some of the freedom they crave, especially once they've been trained to be off-leash. It not only allows them to do their own things but also shows them that you trust them. You must also respect that you're sharing these public spaces with everyone else—and you can't possibly control everyone and everything that's going on. You might have the greatest faith in your dog, but you can't predict the behaviour of other dogs or their owners.

Even at the dog park, you'll encounter the occasional dog-phobe, human or canine. You'll also encounter the occasional jerk who seems to be looking for trouble. We know the expression "misery loves company," and sometimes it seems that people purposely go out to the dog park looking to vent their day's frustrations on innocent bystanders. That person and his or her dog could be an accident waiting to happen. Do your best to read people and their dogs before they come into close proximity. Make eye contact and say hello. That's not only a good ice breaker; it also helps you determine whether they're open to engaging with you and your dog or are fearful, reluctant or a potential troublemaker.

Be constantly mindful of your own dog's body language and of the body language of other people and dogs. If you get the all clear from all parties involved, invite human conversation while the dogs greet each other and determine for themselves whether they click. If your dog is leashed, relax your hold while the dogs are doing the meet and greet. Yanking them backwards makes them feel stifled and sends the message that you don't think they can be trusted. As I mentioned earlier, I've noticed that most dog fights occur when either both or one of the dogs is leashed. I've rarely seen fights break out between two unleashed dogs, and I think that says a lot about the fact that when dogs are allowed the time and space to speak to each other in their own language, using their own innate doggy social rules, they rarely square off against each other.

Some dogs will yap a little when they play. Bisco did this because she was such a social butterfly. She wasn't signalling aggression; she was just socially clueless and was feeling constricted by a tight leash. If you notice that your dog's yapping intensifies, remove him from the situation. Ditto if your dog or another dog starts to nip while playing. If your dog was the offender, use a leash correction, find a bench and put your dog in a sit-stay for at least ten minutes.

———

HUMPING HOUNDS

This one really cracks me up, because people get so embarrassed. Anybody who's spent any time in a dog park knows that dogs will sometimes try to get it on with their neighbourhood dog buddies, and many will gladly engage in the human equivalent of a one-night stand. Some people try to break their dogs up when they do this, but I think it should be permitted as long as your dog isn't objecting. They're not necessarily engaging in sexual behaviour. Sometimes they're just playing and wrestling around. Sometimes they're trying to show that they're top dog, and if that other dog consents, why is it our business to step in their way? On the other hand, sometimes the behaviour *is* sexually motivated. Dogs, just like humans, also masturbate, whether they've been fixed or not. Get over it, humans, and let dogs be dogs.

Off-Leash Training

Bisco, the party animal, often let her enthusiasm and excitement get the better of her, so I mixed up her training with a lot of play. But if she continued to blow me off, breaking a sit or stay, I'd tie her to a tree so she'd realize that her privilege to mix with the other dogs would be removed if she didn't become more patient with training. She started to realize that she'd have to be accountable for her behaviour before she earned the right to go off-leash.

It took about six months to prepare Bisco for off-leash training, but the length of time it will take you and your dog will depend on the dog's personality and on the amount and quality of the time you've spent on basic training. Here's the stage that you and your dog should be at before you start off-leash training:

1. You've developed your power to dictate all movement during umbilical. Your dog is always looking at you and respects your lead position. Whenever you walk together, the leash is relaxed.

2. When you walk together with the leash draped over your hand, it doesn't slip off your hand.

3. When you drop the leash to the ground, your dog continues to walk with you, by your side. When you move faster, change directions or stop, your dog moves and stops with you. If your dog bolts away at this point, you will need to do more work building up your bond and developing all the skill sets I've already discussed.

4. When you remove the leash altogether and repeat the drill described in points 1 to 3 (above), the dog is still making eye contact, still moving with you and doesn't need repeated commands to stop.

Off-Leash Sit, Stay, Come and Stop

The initial phase of off-leash sit and stay training is just like the sit and stay training I outlined in the previous chapter, except that it should be done outdoors. You'll need space, so start off-leash training in a park if possible. If that freaks you out too much, find an enclosed outdoor spot like a tennis court. Keep the dog leashed up, but let the leash drag on the ground so if she attempts to bolt, you can step on the leash. Your dog should be able to sit and stay for twenty minutes, and when you say, "Stop," she should be able to stop on a dime.

The off-leash come or hustle command is a bit more advanced. Here's how to do it:

* Place your dog in a stay for one minute.
* Back up about five feet or so (about one and a half metres) and then say, "Come" or "Hustle" as you turn and start running away from your dog.
* As soon as the dog catches up to you, turn quickly and start running in the opposite direction. The goal is to get your dog to follow you whenever and wherever you go.
* Repeat the exercise one more time and then give your dog a really good chest scrunch.
* Repeat again, but this time, add about five feet (about one and a half metres) between you and your dog.
* Repeat the process, adding five more feet of distance between you and your dog each time until there's a twenty-foot (about six-metre) distance between you and your dog. Don't rush through this training. People sometimes don't do enough off-leash training work, and this could lead to a tragedy.

After the come or hustle command is mastered, you'll be ready to learn off-leash road crossing—the ultimate safeguard for your dog.

* Find a low-traffic street that has a good, long-distance sightline so you can monitor approaching traffic.
* Do some refresher sit-stay exercises near the curb of the street.
* Now cross the road together and do another sit-stay on the opposite curb.
* On the next crossing, let the leash drop on the

ground. Your dog should be by your side for the entire crossing and, she should be able to sit-stay on command once you get to the curb.

* Repeat the exercise at least six times, mixing up your pace so your dog follows your lead and is paying attention to you no matter what the speed.

* I'll bet you'll be completely stoked once you can do this exercise many times successfully—and you'll deserve to be! It's an awesome achievement for both you and your dog, and your dog deserves a good dose of praise. But it's a bad idea to start shrieking and hollering and getting overexcited. Celebrate your success with a good rip (run) in the park.

* The next time you do the exercise, try it with the leash in your pocket.

* Gradually start putting a little distance between yourself and the dog. If your dog picks up a scent in the middle of the road and gets distracted for a second, that's fine—it's a chance for you to use your verbal command or another signal to get your dog to come—as long as she responds immediately.

It took a while to get Bisco to stop meandering and losing focus during our training. She had to be able to sit on that first snap and come on that first whistle call, Cathy and Jim's preferred signals. And even though I'd been working with Bisco off-leash for a while, Cathy's first few off-leash attempts didn't exactly play like a dream.

"The first time I set out to do it, I was so nervous the entire walk to the off-leash park," admits Cathy, who brought a friend for backup. "As soon as I let go of the leash and she started to run, I panicked and immediately started calling her name over and over. It was like a self-fulfilling prophecy. I said to my friend, 'Oh, I should never have gotten a dog!'" Cathy's friend bolted after Bisco and no harm was done. In fact, the whole turn of events steeled Cathy's determination to make training *herself* in off-leash a top priority. "I knew I had to train me." Cathy's reaction was helpful because she was weaning herself from her fears by being determined to try again. I trusted that Bisco could go off-leash, but by falling back on her old habit of being untrusting of Bisco and then overusing emotionally charged, high-pitched verbal commands, Cathy failed herself and her dog. But she didn't dwell on that mistake. She persevered.

"Now I have no fears when she's off-leash," says Cathy. "Seeing her run and frolic gives me such joy. I swear she looks like she's smiling. Those are really Zen moments. I know I'm meeting her needs and I don't have to worry about chasing her around and watching her like a hawk, because she's always watching me. We enjoy each other's company. She's a gift, not a liability.

"If we're short on time and can only do an hour romp, Jim drops us off and drives to the other side of the park. I'll say, 'Get the chief,' and she'll run to Jim. Then he'll say, 'Get the chief,' and she'll run back and forth, and we both feel great when we come home. I trust her with other dogs and also with the grandkids because she's satisfied and secure in herself."

Socializing with Kids

Even if you don't have kids in your life, you're going to meet them at the dog park. Obviously, if you *do* have kids of your own, your dog may already know how to mix with other children. If not, it's best to introduce your dog to kids inside your home, so you have maximum control.

Once you start mixing outdoors, you'll be dealing with unpredictable situations and any number of kids, so always stick with your dog. When a child approaches, do your best to gauge the child's mood and then give clear instructions about the way your dog likes to be engaged before that child so much as reaches out a hand toward your dog. Some of the mellowest dogs don't like to be petted in certain places, so provide kids with general pointers from the start. If kid-dog contact is involved, stay with your dog, getting down on your haunches to be at eye level with both of them, positioning your body at a forty-five-degree angle to your pooch. The same goes if you have your own kids with you and they want to meet other dogs. They should already know how to mix safely with dogs, but you should always ask the dog owner whether the stranger dog is comfortable and safe with kids before you let your child interact with that dog.

Sometimes you'll come across babies or young children in strollers, and in situations like that, I recommend leashing up your dog, particularly if the baby or young child is wailing. Dogs are often drawn to crying babies and children because they interpret them as wounded animals, and their instinct is to put an end to that misery. This can lead to tragedy, so you must handle the situation with care. Don't panic, but instead *calmly* grab the leash and lead your dog away from the crying baby or child. If the baby or child is quiet and the parent wants to engage with you, be extra-vigilant about your dog's behaviour and body language and never ever let your dog poke his head into a baby's stroller. If you have your own kids, your dog should already know that the stroller is off limits, but other dogs might not, so if you're the one with the baby or child and stroller in tow, don't assume that unknown dogs have been taught the rules of engagement.

Dog Fights

If a dog fight breaks out, there'll be little or no time to react. Dogs move so much faster than humans, so in many cases, the damage is done before the humans have any time to think. If a dog fight does break out, don't start screaming in a high-pitched, emotionally charged voice. That's the worst thing you can do because the dogs will read that as a sign of weakness, and that could make them more aggressive with each other. You might be able to break the fight up by yelling in a deep, confident voice. But if that doesn't work, don't make any further effort to break up the fight. There are just too many variables involved in a situation like this. Police train for months to learn how to break up human fights, and it would be a mistake to treat dog fights any differently. These professionals practise these scenarios over and over again to train themselves how to move quickly and to know what to do in a variety of specific situations. I've been working with dogs for twenty years, and I use many different techniques to break up dog fights or handle aggressive dogs. Last year, I was working with an extremely aggressive dog, and I was prepared to give up my right arm if he attacked. Then if he started to make lunch out of it, I could grab his collar with my free hand and close off his air supply to force him to release my arm. Luckily, the situation never became that heated, but to break up a dog fight, you have to be willing to put yourself on the line—and even then, you could pay with your life and your dog's.

My best advice is this: if dogs are fighting, leave them alone! But if you do step in instinctively before you realize you shouldn't have, here are a few pointers to keep you out of more trouble:

* Never put your body between the two dogs, not even a hand. That would be like sticking your hand in a blender: you'll get bitten simply because your hand is in the way.
* If the dog is clamped onto the other dog, do not attempt to rip them apart.
* Step aside calmly as soon as you can (without making the dogs more upset) and yell, "Back off!" in a very deep voice. Call a trained professional for assistance, if possible, and let that professional do the work of breaking up the fight if they feel that is wise.

Meeting Senior Citizens

I once met a woman in the dog park who said she believed her dog had a fear of elderly people, especially those who used canes or walkers. The usually placid little pooch would sometimes even growl and bare his teeth at seniors. Because of that, the woman believed her dog's previous owner had been an elderly person who had abused the dog. Whenever his ears perked up or he started to growl, the woman would scoop him into her arms and comfort him, but this actually encouraged the bad behaviour.

Was there really an elderly villain in this dog's history? Dogs who've been beaten will develop phobias, as in the case of a Mexican dog I met in Vancouver who had a phobia of umbrellas. (Considering all the rain, Vancouver's a bad place for that kind of phobia.) It's not likely that the dog in question had been beaten. It's more probable that he was actually picking up on seniors' slower body movements and the physical frailties and unusual gait of people who need to walk with assistance. That's why the elderly rank second-highest (after kids) among victims of dog bites.

It was cool to see the light bulb go on for this woman once she understood these simple facts about body movement. It's one of the many reasons that providing your dog with a lot of variety and introducing her to as many situations as possible is so important. That way, if she sees a new type of movement, she won't be thrown by it, since she'll be accustomed to seeing many different human gaits and ways of moving around.

If a real phobia does develop, it can be hard to kick. I recommend slowly introducing the dog to that trigger, whether it's an umbrella or a wheelchair. I did this with a dog who went ballistic around chainsaws—with the chainsaw *off*, of course! I slowly inched toward the dog with the chainsaw in my hands and when he appeared calm, he came right up to the chainsaw, sniffed it for a minute or so and realized it wasn't a threat. Some dogs are sensitive to certain noises, in which case I recommend the same process of starting off from a distance, gradually moving the dog as close to the source of the noise as would truly be safe and being wary of any signs of anxiety, such as shaking, chewing or spinning. I thought that when I went back to work, he might start barking again, but he didn't. If your dog continues to bark or act out because of a phobia connected with a certain sound or specific situation, say, "Leave it." Be careful of your own body language and do your best to mask any of your own anxiety by keeping your shoulders back and at least faking a confident stature. Be sensitive to triggers by not placing your dog in situations where they might occur until the dog no longer has the phobia. But don't let your dog get away with rude or aggressive behaviours caused by a phobic reaction.

Socialites versus Homebodies

Remember, doggy temperament is not so much about the breed; it's about the personality of your dog. Some dogs don't like to be more than six feet (about two metres) from their owners; other dogs can have a thirty-foot (about nine-metre) comfort zone. All dogs are different and there's so much cross-breeding now that choosing a dog based on breed isn't reliable. Some dogs are wired on life and need a ton of exercise; others are lounge-a-lots, content to sit around and watch the butterflies. Some dogs I know are very social animals and others could take or leave other dogs. It's not necessarily a negative thing for a dog to be a loner as long as the dog has had enough exposure to other dogs and is *choosing* to be aloof. Peggy and Steve's Australian shepherd, Rocky, and Spencer, Hartley's golden retriever, are more interested in engaging humans than dogs. My dog Dez loved to go to the dog park, but once she was there, she often preferred to kick back on the sidelines to people-watch and dog-watch. Rudy and Mia are party animals and always want to be in the mix

By fulfilling your dog's basic need for exercise and mental stimulation and exposing him to a variety of situations and adventures, you'll have a much richer understanding of your dog's unique personality, and he'll be free to express his true nature.

———

Outdoor Safety

It's important to provide your dog with many different kinds of outdoor exercise, but the dog's safety must always come first. If you live in a hot climate or your area gets hot during the dog days of summer, take your pooch out for walks in the early morning or evening so she doesn't overheat. And *never* leave your dog unattended in a hot car. Signs that your dog is too hot include excessive panting, heavier breathing, seeking out shade, digging as if trying to find cooler ground and gummy saliva that whitens the dog's tongue. If you're going on a marathon hike, make sure to bring extra water for your dog, and if there are cacti or nettles underfoot that could sting or prickle the skin, consider booties to protect your dog's paws. Choose locations near streams or lakes so your dog can take a dip to cool off, but be mindful of currents, water levels and debris that could injure your animal. During the winter months, it's best to avoid frozen lakes and streams just in case your dog falls through the ice.

In colder climates, all breeds, but especially short-haired ones, might need a winter coat and booties to ward off frostbite. Use common sense to decide whether the temperature is too cold outside and also look for cues from your dog, such as if he is shivering or keeps picking her paws up off the ground. A coat and booties will also protect dogs when the streets are covered in salt and other harsh chemicals, which can wreak havoc with their sensitive paws and underbellies. They'll also be tempted to lick the salt off, so if your dog doesn't need a coat and boots to stay warm, prevent her from ingesting these chemicals by rinsing her paws and belly when you get home.

No matter what the climate, when you're going off-leash,

be sure to keep the leash handy in case you come across an aggressive dog or other animals. Be vigilant about everything going on around you, especially if you're out camping in the wilderness or in big, open spaces. I once saw an eagle snatch a little dog off a Vancouver beach. That horrifying incident is burned into my brain, and I hope you don't have to see such a tragedy to appreciate that you have to be watchful of your dog and the surrounding environment at all times.

Car Safety

When you're taking your dog out in a car, she'll often get hyperactive in anticipation, thinking that you're headed for the dog park or a big nature rip, even if you're just going out for coffee. That excitement is natural, but it could lead to disaster once you get to your destination and your dog bounds out of the car in a parking lot. As you get ready to go on a car trip (no matter how long or short), make sure your dog is leashed before you step out the front door. Don't let her charge into the back of the truck or climb into the vehicle before you're ready to go. Your driveway might be relatively safe, but with car etiquette, it's vital to maintain consistency, so your dog must learn to follow your commands wherever you are. Once you're outside, if you have time, do some sit-stay training, and once you're ready to go, invite the dog into the car.

Some people choose to buckle their dogs up in the back-seat, and that is a good idea. I usually park my dogs on the backseat floor. We all know that dogs love to stick their heads out the window of a moving vehicle, so they can check out the neighbourhood news and suck up exotic new smells. But that air is also filled with insects and debris that could potentially damage or even blind a dog. It's better to be safe than sorry, so open the windows just a crack to give your dog a fix of new smells, but not enough that her eyes will be endangered.

Once you get to the park, if you're not yet confident that she'll follow the sit-stay rules, leash her up before you open the car door. That way, she won't jump out of the car, bolt toward the park and potentially get hit by another car. Once again, use this time to train your dog to be patient and respectful of your lead role. When it's time to return to the car, leash your dog up again at least fifty yards (about fifty metres) from the parking lot. When you arrive at the car, don't allow your dog to bound into the back. Get her to sit patiently until you're ready to go and then invite her into the vehicle.

It's a good idea to check your dog's paws and fur after an outdoor rip, just in case he picked up any little sticks, stones, burrs or bugs. (I'll provide more tips on dog grooming and health care in Chapter 7.)

City Slickers

It slays me when people say, "How could that apartment dweller have a Husky? It's dog abuse!" Well, a little Jack Russell needs just as much exercise as a Husky—if not more—and putting your dog in the backyard doesn't count for exercise; it's just a slightly bigger cell. You might prefer living in the burbs or a rural spot, but most people still crave the energy and stimulation of the city—and so do many dogs. Research from the University of Southampton in the U.K. has shown that dogs not exposed to urban environments were more likely to have negative traits like avoidance and aggression.

The study found that after six to twelve months, dogs exposed to a wide range of environments were no longer clingy.[31]

It's important to provide your dog with a mixed bag of physical and mental stimulation. So if you're going downtown, take him with you occasionally, so he can sniff out and drink up the exotic sights, sounds, smells and rhythms of a faster-paced environment. You can go for a walk or park yourself on a café patio and enjoy people watching together. If you live in the city, expose your dog to quieter rural parks and woods occasionally to give him a break from hyperstimulating places.

Remember to Rut-Bust

If you're on a strict routine, your dog will know that when you put on the trench coat, it's a workday and she's only getting a quickie morning walk. (No wonder when casual Friday rolls around, she thinks you're going for a walk and cries the blues when she realizes there's no walk coming.) But if you shake up the routine a bit, your dog will be pleasantly surprised and focus more on you. For your Saturday rip, put on the trench instead of the Gore-Tex and say, "Okay let's go." Your dog will be delighted when she realizes she's getting a lot more mileage than the expected ten-minute walk. This might sound like playing around with your dog's head, but it's one of the most fun ways to continually assert your alpha status. And the more varied the scenarios in your dog's life, the more resilient, flexible and adaptive she'll be. Dogs like surprises, just like humans, especially when it comes to physical exercise.

Change up the times and places where you walk your dog, as well as the length of time you spend on a walk. Take him with you while you run errands or go window shopping and take her to pet-friendly stores and business meetings if possible. Any novelty outing will add mental stimulation and allow your dog to experience new sights, sounds and smells.

Recap: Six-Legged Fitness

Exercise is of the utmost importance for dogs, but too often we try to satisfy this primary need with no more than a rushed walk around the block for a bathroom break. Dogs need time to socialize with other dogs and experience the world beyond their neighbourhoods. They also crave the freedom to romp and play off-leash, which is the ultimate way to bond. Here are the key elements for satisfying your dog's fitness and entertainment needs:

* Try to provide your dog with two hours of outdoor action every day. Ideally, that means giving your dog time to run and play with other dogs, but if you're really strapped for time, take your dog with you on errands.
* Do agility exercises with your dog to sharpen her coordination and smarts. (These will also build up your physical prowess, which will strengthen your alpha status.)
* Give your dog time to socialize with other dogs and learn the rules of doggy engagement.
* Do outdoor training to build up your dog's ability to follow your rules and earn the privilege to go off-leash.
* Be aware of how your expectations about your dog (or lack thereof) affect not only your bond with him but also his ability to socialize freely and safely in the world.

CHAPTER SIX

Home-Wrecking Hounds

CHEWING, SHREDDING AND TERRITORIAL WARS

MYTH: A dog who chews, shreds, digs, poops and pees all over the house, engaging in territorial warfare and other disrespectful behaviours, is just a naturally destructive dog.

REALITY CHECK: Dogs need to be taught consistent household rules, but home wreckers are often underexercised, understimulated, lonely or bored, and these destructive habits are merely symptoms of neglect. We teach dogs, like people, how to treat us, and if we're disrespectful of them, they won't respect us.

Chesapeake's Revenge

Half a leather couch, the arm of a La-Z-Boy recliner, a dozen pairs of pants, countless pairs of underwear, six pairs of shoes and boxer's gloves. These were just a few of the things that Chesa, a seven-month-old, home-wrecking Chesapeake Bay retriever, had destroyed by the time I met her. She might have looked like the most adorable little pup in the world, but Chesa was a poop-disturbing, rebellious control freak. "She was completely defiant, bull-headed and very powerful," says her owner, Todd. "I couldn't manage her on the leash. She'd jump up on people, trying to dominate everyone. I wanted a dog I could go anywhere with off-leash. Instead, she dragged me around like a dead goose. I'd been to other trainers who suggested only treats and prong collars. When I met Brad, I was a heartbeat away from getting rid of her."

Chesa was actually a very curious, vivacious and sociable dog. But Todd was so busy working that she often didn't get a walk until midnight. So she wasn't getting enough exercise, and she was bored, lonely and trying to create some sort of stimulation in her environment to keep from going stir-crazy. By trashing the house every day, she was saying, "You're not giving me what I need, so I'll take something of yours." And she had all day to get creative about home wrecking. That kind of disrespect can lead to serious obsessive behaviours that can be really challenging to fix—like territorial aggressions. But luckily, Todd was willing to commit to a training program with the dual purpose of meeting both species' needs.

I'll walk you through the indoor umbilical and sit-stay training exercises I gave Todd to satisfy Chesa's doggy needs for exercise, mental stimulation and bonding. I chose exercises that could be wedged into Todd's busy schedule, like playing a game of tug-o'-war to help Chesa learn how to play without destroying everything that came near her mouth. The exercises also helped Todd establish house rules of conduct, but to help teach Chesa how to respect his possessions, I showed Todd techniques to help his dog learn what was off limits and what was within bounds. I also taught him methods that would help Chesa appreciate that if she kept trashing the joint, there would be consequences for her actions.

Even good dog citizens sometimes turn to house trashing if there are household changes, such as a new partner or a baby or if everyone has moved to new, unfamiliar turf and the humans haven't had the time to meet the dog's basic needs. Anything that affects the human family—death, illness, divorce, kids going away to college—will also affect the dog. The best ways to avoid stressing your pooch out are to assert and maintain your alpha leadership, refrain from using her as an emotional crutch and, as much as possible, meet the dog's primary needs for exercise, socialization and mental stimulation.

Dogs might also act out when a thunderstorm makes them anxious, when the moon is full or when they're in a new place, like a hotel room. The best way to curb these occasional negative behaviours is to steer clear of strict routines and expose your dog to all kinds of different experiences as much as possible, from an early age.

A perfect canine storm happens when there's a combination of a bunch of factors such as the ones I mentioned above. If your dog is a home wrecker, it's imperative to address that bad behaviour immediately or as soon as you find the mess. Let the dog know that his behaviour was unacceptable and that he's accountable for his actions. People often say that a dog doesn't remember what he did an hour or a day ago, but how does a dog know that when his owner puts on a specific hat, they're going for a walk? How do my dogs remember which paths to take when we go hiking?

Take the dog back to the scene of the crime and say, "What is this? You do not wreck my stuff," in a firm tone. Immediately after showing the dog that you're aware of the destruction, you could also use a timeout method of discipline (see Chapter 4) to show the dog that there are consequences for such actions. But ultimately *you* need to acknowledge your part in the destructiveness and take actions to improve the dog's life. First and foremost, asserting your leadership is key to raising a dog who respects you and your property. Daily exercise and socialization time will also curb the dog's boredom and anxiety. And as I mentioned in the previous chapter, dogs also crave new stimuli and variety in their lives. The sky's the limit when it comes to the many ways you can bond with your dog and create a mutually respectful relationship. But that can't happen if you live in a chaotic environment and spend the majority of your precious time together yelling at your dog for misconduct.

Alpha Turf Wars

If you don't train your dog to understand that you're the boss, imagine how she's going to react when some new interloper shows up and she has to play sharesies with said complete stranger. I've met a number of Frankendogs who are simply reacting to environmental changes, like a new partner. If the owner *and* the new partner are both unaware of the need to assert their alpha positions, it just means I have to train one more person to assume leadership over the dog. But nine times out of ten, I'm called in when the new partner refuses to be bossed around by Four Legs and this newcomer and the dog are duking it out for the family crown. The dog becomes a potential relationship deal breaker. The walking papers are ready, but it's just not certain which party will be shown the door.

How would you expect the dog to react to an entirely new set of rules, especially if she's assumed the CEO position? She's probably been feeling snubbed ever since the new boyfriend showed up one Friday night and ruined the usual long petting session on the couch. And she's likely thinking, "Mom's been distracted ever since she kicked me out of *my* bed that fateful night. She doesn't have as much time for me and has gone and changed all the rules." A spoiled alpha dog like that is naturally going to take it out on the new arrival. She's going to say, "Heh, I'll show you" and purposely target the new tyrant's stuff. When the new friend comes to his new home and finds his stuff trashed, he freaks and unleashes ultimatums on the partner. The partner yells back and cries and a real-life soap opera follows. Meanwhile, the dog just sits there with her head cocked innocently to the side, thinking, "Wow, all that bad behaviour actually gets me a good chunk of attention! Better start planning for tomorrow's blitz."

To avoid these alpha power struggles, make sure your dog is well trained to know that Two Legs is household boss before any changes occur in the environment. If that doesn't happen, don't be surprised when the newbie joining the ranks puts his or her foot down and insists that your dog needs to be trained to know who's in charge. At that point, it's imperative for the entire family to work as a team to ensure a smooth transition.

Let Sleeping Dogs Lie (In Their Own Beds)

I'll discuss the dangers of the ways people humanize dogs in more detail in the next chapter. But if your dog has boundary and respect issues or if you anticipate that there will be life changes in your future, the best way to stop or avoid home-wrecking behaviours is to make sure to train your pooch so he knows what's off limits and what's allowed in the home. That means making all human furniture, especially your own bed, off limits for four-legged family members.

A pet that sleeps with his owner is vulnerable to alpha problems, jealousy issues, territory-related aggressions (especially when you introduce new humans into the mix) and separation anxiety. I'll give you advice on how to train your dog not to chomp on the furniture in a minute, but first, one thing needs to be clear: you must provide your dog with a space of his own, where he can retreat when there's a lot of human commotion or when he wants to retire for a nap or bedtime. That oasis could be an outdoor doghouse, a dog run in the backyard or an indoor zone, well away from the commotion, like a dog crate or a dog bed with plenty of space around it just for Rover. Note that the area must be warm, clean and dry. Avoid cold basement floors or tiled floors or put an effective heat-retaining barrier between your dog's bed and any cold surface.

When you're shopping for a dog bed, opt for low-maintenance ones that can be washed regularly and have about six inches of buffer to give the dog enough space to stretch out.

The dog's area should be off limits to humans, and show respect for the dog's space by keeping it clean and free of human clutter. If you demonstrate respect for your dog's belongings, he'll be encouraged to respect yours. And if he still goes ahead and ruins your things, you'll have to correct the behaviour. Whether you catch him in the act of trashing your stuff or not, take the item away as soon as you notice it's being or has been wrecked. Then (still at the scene of destruction), show the dog the trashed item and say, "Leave it" in a firm tone. Then put one of your dog's toys in front of him, to encourage him to play with his own things.

Teaching "Bed"

Whatever your choice for a dog bed, introduce your dog to it by saying, "This is your bed" in an enthusiastic but non-high-pitched tone. Then get her to lie down on the bed by saying, "Go to bed." When she lies down, say, "Good buddy," call her back to you, give her a chest scrunch and repeat the request again until she understands that this is *her* spot. You can do the same thing if you have a specific place for your dog to chill out in your living area, like a rug. With specific locations and phrases, you can verbally command your dog to relax or steer clear of certain zones where you might not want your dog to be, such as the kitchen while you're preparing dinner. With these boundaries and instructions, she'll know her place in the household.

Chewing and Shredding

Puppies go through a natural teething stage, just like babies. An adult chewer might have separation anxiety issues, which I'll get into in the next chapter, but she might also have trouble deciphering what's off limits. You can help your dog learn these boundaries and also help her stave off boredom simply by playing with her, using her favourite toys. If she starts playing with one of your possessions instead, say, "Leave it " and give her one of her own toys. Your dog should have no more than three toys. If there are too many toys around and they're all mixed up among the humans' belongings, your dog won't know what she should and shouldn't chew.

I'll give you more tips on how to find the right toys for

your dog in Chapter 7, but here's a sneak preview. Good toys that help with teething puppies and bored dogs include uncooked beef bone (from the butcher or grocery store, not the pet store) and strong rope (which at the hardware store costs about 10 per cent of what pet stores charge). I'm also a firm believer in taking a rag or an old towel and playing tug-o'-war with the dog. It's great for dogs who are teething and also for providing mental stimulation. One myth going around is that you shouldn't play tug-o'-war because it will teach a dog to be aggressive. But dogs often play tug with each other without lapsing into dangerous behaviour. It actually helps them improve their social skills and understand that there are rules even when it comes time to play.

The Ouch Test

To help train your dog to play safe and release toys and other objects on command, I'll walk you through a simple exercise. Remember that you should always supervise any play between small kids and dogs and, as I've said before, children should never be left alone with dogs. Do this exercise many times when the kids aren't around to make sure your dog responds consistently to your ouch tests.

* Get down on the floor with your dog and his favourite chew toy or bone.
* Give the toy or bone to your dog.
* Say, "Ouch" in a high-pitched tone. (This is the one situation where I endorse using such a tone, so make it count!)
* If the dog doesn't let go of the toy or bone, pinch his ear so he let's out an ouch-like, high-pitched sound and releases immediately.
* Now start again. This time, when you say, "Ouch," the dog should release. If not, continue doing the exercise until he releases as soon as you say, "Ouch."
* If your dog doesn't release on "Ouch," say, "Release right now. This will not be tolerated" in a firm voice.

This simple exercise not only teaches your dog to release an object on command; it also acknowledges that you know what it means when the dog says, "Ouch." But if your tone of voice isn't high-pitched enough or if you don't say, "Ouch" quickly enough, the dog may not let go. It's especially good training to do this with the dog's bone, so he knows he should relinquish food of any kind to anybody. The key to the entire exercise is being consistent and staying on top of the training. If at a given time, your dog doesn't relinquish the bone, you must take it from him—and be firm about it. If you are training a puppy, you could hold it by the scruff of its neck, as a mother does with her pups. But remember to be gentle.

I'd prefer that you keep the words to a minimum and use actions instead, but as long as you've gone through the no talking for two weeks initial training and continue to limit your talk to very basic commands and phrases, words can be an effective disciplining method—as long as you remember to keep your tone firm. With consistent training about rules and boundaries, you'll avoid possessive or territorial aggressions.

PLAY CUES

*A*ccording to a University of California study, dogs engaged in "rough-and-tumble" play sent subtle signals that they most often wanted to play with partners who were facing them. When a partner faced away and was inattentive, the dogs engaged in "attention-getting behaviours" and "acted to manipulate" the person or dog to play with them.[32]

Eliminating Elimination Issues

Anybody who's potty-trained a child knows that the process can be challenging and success can take years, depending on your individual child. Same goes for dogs. It's imperative that you start house training your pup immediately. And same goes if you've inherited a non-trained adult dog. Elimination issues sometimes also develop in later years, necessitating re-training, but they can also result from significant life changes or neglect.

Pups will have accidents in the early stages of training, and I'll discuss that in more detail in Chapter 9. Accidents happen with adult dogs as well if you neglect to give them the necessary morning and evening bathroom breaks outside. Dogs can hold their bladders through the night—and often for longer than eight hours on weekends, when the Two Legs sleep in. They should also be able to hold through an eight-hour workday if you give them a decent morning bathroom break before you head off to work. But if you've provided enough breaks and you're still constantly coming home to a pile of turd on your living room floor, the dog is probably exhibiting home-wrecking behaviours.

If the adult home wrecker does the deal inside the house, whether it was two minutes ago or two days ago, it's imperative that you discipline her. Just as for other home-wrecking behaviours, dogs do remember what they've done for quite some time after the fact. Here's how to tell them not to do such things again:

* Take your dog back to the scene.
* Tell him in a calm, deep tone that his behaviour was unacceptable.
* Give him the silent treatment for at least fifteen minutes: don't talk to him and don't look at him. Completely ignore him for that period of time so he understands the deed was unacceptable.

Wild dogs pee and poop to mark their territory, and domestic dogs will do the same if they haven't been properly trained to understand your house rules or if they've developed territorial behavioural problems. Back in Chapter 2, I mentioned the success Jenn had in house training her miniature golden doodle, Jackson, while he was on umbilical training. This also works with adult dogs who've developed elimination issues.

If you're meeting all your dog's needs and accidents are still happening, I recommend that you do this very simple exercise:

* Keep a journal for a week to ten days, writing down the times the dog pees and poops. That way, you can calculate how long the dog can hold her bladder (perhaps eighty-five to a hundred minutes).
* Put the dog on umbilical and keep busy, so she has to hold her bladder.
* Once you exceed the initial average by ten to twenty minutes, take her outside and see if she has to go to the bathroom.
* Did she go? Make sure you praise your dog by saying, "Good pee" or "Good poo."
* Repeat this exercise as often as you can and be on the lookout for any signs that your dog might use to indicate she needs a bathroom break. (Remember that once she's full grown, your dog should be able to hold her bladder for eight hours.)

Put your dog's journal on the fridge door or in some other easily accessible place, so that anyone in the household can write down the times your dog has had a bathroom break. This keeps all family members involved in teaching responsibility, and that has a payoff for everyone.

Chesa: Dog Interrupted

It took a lot of hard work to get Chesa down from her one-armed La-Z-Boy throne. But Todd committed himself to the training program, starting with the umbilical and no talking rule. "We went on a lot of walks, and at first she pulled like crazy because I admit she hadn't been getting enough exercise and socialization time with other dogs," says Todd. "I got cut marks from her trying to drag me around, but I persisted. We did agility training, weaving in and out of trees and also did the group training so she could learn how to be social without jumping up at everything that moved."

Interrupting Jumping Up

Interrupting a dog from jumping up at people or on furniture is actually quite easy: throw your hand down toward the dog's face really fast, with your palm flat and facing the dog. The dog will think, "If I jump up, I'll run into that hand." This method is effective and nonintrusive. It's not effective to push a dog around or, worse, knee the dog in the chest. Neither action stops the jumping up behaviour. When a dog is pushed, the action isn't fast enough to get the message across, and kneeing (especially when it's a reflex reaction) could actually maim or kill the dog. Because the bones in a dog's chest are only about a quarter inch thick (a bit more than half a centimetre thick), you could break your dog's ribs or collapse his chest by kneeing.

The hand throwdown also works with pooches that mooch at the dinner table. But remember, if you're not fast enough or not consistent and the dog manages to jump up, you'll need to discipline her. First, grab her by the collar and pull her off the furniture, person or table edge as quickly as you possibly can. If she tries to jump up again, interrupt her movement with the hand throwdown technique. If she continues to try jumping up, you must persevere and make sure *you* score the win. Don't let your dog play the "Poor me" card, whining and pulling a hangdog face. That just means she's attempting manipulation to beat you at the game. If your dog keeps jumping up or if she tries manipulating you, put her in a timeout and give her the cold shoulder.

Todd used the same methods when Chesa shred the blanket in her crate during the initial umbilical phase. He put her in her timeout zone—a doorknob rigged on a short leash that didn't allow her to lie down—and said in a firm, deep tone, "What is this? Do not wreck your stuff." Then he left her in jail for about twenty minutes. While she was in that timeout, he didn't speak to her, look at her or acknowledge her presence, so she understood the gravity of the situation.

Interrupting and correcting her behaviours at home was critical, but so was building up their bond and introducing structure to Chesa's life. Todd did a lot of sit-stay training at home. "We'd circle around the house, and at first I had to use the leash to get her to sit," says Todd. "But after only a few of those, I could snap to get her to sit every few steps, then build it up to twenty paces." Sounds easy, right? But a control freak's behaviours don't disappear overnight. Training Chesa to consistently follow commands was still very challenging and really pushed the patience envelope of both species. "Sometimes it seemed pointless trying to teach her to stay and stop," admits Todd. "Other dogs in the group had it lock, stock and barrel without much effort. But we had to do a lot of work."

I remember hanging out at Todd's home office while he was going through that process about a month after training began. Todd was trying to teach Chesa to stay lying down while he worked at his computer. But she kept getting back up and walking out the door, so he had to run after her, bring her back and say, "Lie down." Then she'd get back up and the process had to be repeated many times. I told him to leash her up, so when she started to move, he could put his foot down on the leash. I'll never forget how she looked at him: "Dammit! How'd you figure that one out?"

We also did "stop" training but used a thirty-foot (about nine-metre) leash so Chesa couldn't bolt from the proverbial schoolyard. The long leash allowed her room for movement, but if she took off after some furry critter or another dog, we could grab the leash and stop her. Three months later, she was off-leashed trained. "I wanted a dog I could go anywhere with and now I have that dog," says Todd.

Most importantly, Todd had to learn that he was too busy to meet Chesa's doggy needs for exercise and a social life. He had to network to establish a life for her while he was busy working, including dog walkers and friends of both species that she could hang out with if he had to work late.

Training Couch Potatoes

Some people just love to laze around on the couch. How people spend their leisure time is none of my business, but for some strange reason, many of these couch potatoes want their dogs right there, snuggled up beside them. Then there's a visit from someone who's allergic, dog-phobic or wearing a penguin suit en route to a formal event—and all of a sudden that teli-tubby dog isn't allowed on the couch. There's an easy solution, to prevent confusion: don't let your dog up on the furniture or in your human bed at any time. If you must have your dog beside you while you watch TV, get down on the floor with him.

If your pooch needs to be trained out of lounging all over the furniture, you will have to interrupt and discipline him in order to institute new boundaries. I can hear some of you saying, "Oh, Brad, I don't want to hurt my dog." Oh, but do you think the mixed messages aren't hurting him? Once again, this is where consistency comes in. If you're constantly changing the rules, your dog will find it impossible to understand you, and that's just an invitation for your dog to tune you out.

Busting Boredom: Home Is Where the Heart and Mind Are

Just like kids, dogs need a lot of mental stimulation, not just to keep them busy and to fight boredom but also to satisfy their desire to learn, work and have a sense of purpose in their lives. If your dog is engaging in home-wrecking behaviours, he's probably bored and trying to create some sort of stimulation to keep from going barmy. Good thinking games will fill that void.

In all the previous chapters, I've talked about various ways you can inject mental stimulation into you dog's daily physical exercises but you can and should also play thinking games at home. If your dog engages in bad behaviours at home, playing games is an excellent way to curb any negative emotions she has around the house. This also lets her know that her needs for mental stimulation can be provided in-house, not just when you set foot outside. We don't put our kids' learning activities and playtime on hold when they have to stay inside, and we shouldn't do that with our dogs either.

Playing Hide-and-Seek

Hide-and-seek is a great way to get your dog thinking. You can play the game just as you do with kids, but with the dog playing the seeker. This satisfies dogs who lust to do search-related work, and it also gives you an opportunity to play and offer a reward for a job well done. When your dog finds you, he'll be all jazzed up, and that will be a great reward in itself!

I also do a variation on the game by hiding three of the dog's favourite toys, such as a bone or a stick, a ball, a squeaky or plush toy or a rope toy. By doing this, you'll be encouraging your dog to chew and play with appropriate items instead of your human off-limits possessions. Here's how to play this game:

* Spread the dog's three favourite toys around on the floor and give each of them a simple name. Get down on the ground, pick up each toy and say its name out loud a few times. Now you've created a vocabulary for the dog that gets her thinking and paying attention to you.

* Stand back and ask your dog to fetch each of the toys, one at a time.

* Once your dog can differentiate between the names of the toys, command her to sit.

* Choose one of the toys, repeat the name of that toy and then take it into another room and hide it Come back to the dog and say, "Find rope" or "Seek rope." You may or may not have to point to the other room before the dog understands that she should go looking there.

* Give your dog some time to find the toy and bring it back to you.

* Praise your dog verbally or with a good chest scrunch.

* Repeat the process with the second toy.

* Then repeat the process again with the third toy.

* Once your dog gets the hang of hide-and-seek with

one toy, add a second toy to the game. Hold up and name the first toy. Then do the same with the second toy.

* Before you leave the room to hide one of the toys, make sure your dog sees that you have both toys.
* Hide the second toy and put the first toy in your pocket or stash it somewhere out of the dog's reach.
* When you return to the dog, ask her to find the second item.
* Once your dog has success with the second item, show her the first and second toys again, naming each one as you hold it up. Then hide both toys in the other room. Come back and tell her to find only one of the toys. See if she can discern between the requested toy and the other hidden toy. It could take a while for the dog to understand the word tags for each toy.

Some dogs—particularly dogs who need a lot of repetition—respond more slowly than others to word tags like "Seek rope," so be patient, and if you start getting frustrated, or if your dog doesn't seem interested, don't push it. Stop playing and try again some other time. Never judge your dog the first few times you play these types of games. He might simply be tired or he might be more interested in getting some outdoor physical exercise with you. But don't give up on the mental games. The more you play them, the sharper your dog's skill set will become.

If you're really strapped for time and can't play a good stimulation game, do some umbilical while you do your own chores or even kick back to relax. This is the easiest way to put your dog into an attentive and mentally stimulated state.

DOGGY VOCABULARY

*I*n order to be street-safe and to understand house-hold rules, dogs should be able to understand at least twenty words. The words themselves don't matter as long as they're connected to a certain command or expected behaviour. Here are some common words and simple phrases that your dog should know: sit, stay, stop, come, hustle, lie down (or rug—or whatever place you've assigned as her chill-out spot), bed, food, leave it (or, instead, don't or no), it's okay (meaning "chill out already"), good, awesome (or some similar word to show enthusiasm and praise for good behaviour), hi, goodbye (or some sort of bonjour and adieu), car or truck, watch the car (so the dog feels useful when you have to leave her in the car for a short time—with the window open a crack, don't forget!) and the names of three toys (such as ball, stick and rope).

Speaking of vocabulary, according to research at the Germany-based Max Planck Institute for Evolutionary Anthropology, a Border collie named Rico was able to recognize the names of over two hundred items and retrieve those specific toys. Seventy per cent of the time, Rico could differentiate between a known and an unknown item. He could also learn new names for new items and remember the name of that new item in later tests. Kids also learn this important cognitive ability, called "fast mapping," [33] and the researchers noted that domestic dogs are "unusually skilled at reading human social and communicative behaviour."[34]

Home or Away for the Holidays

Dogs will sometimes degenerate into demon-like behaviour during holidays like Christmas and Rosh Hashanah. It might seem that your dog is purposely trying to make the season miserable by trashing the house, but your pet's negative behaviour is likely the result of the sudden changes that happen in holiday seasons, causing stress for everyone, human and canine. Picture the home suddenly mobbed with overexcited relatives, including bratty nieces and nephews, the son who just flunked out of college and the monster-in-law, who's packed a superiority complex and a couple of spoiled-rotten, four-legged creatures. You might have anticipated the perfect Norman Rockwell season, but things can turn downright grinchy when the high expectations we heap on holidays are disappointed.

Dogs don't believe in the Easter Bunny or Santa, but far too often they receive gifts of coal in the form of stress, noise, tense human vibes and human neglect of their primary needs. They're also prone to getting the wrong kind of attention, and sometimes abuse, from kids and elderly people whose rules differ from yours.

Add decorations to that family sideshow setting and you've got a giant booby trap: electrical cords everywhere inviting chewing and electrocution; shiny baubles that could easily break and turn to deadly shards; plants like mistletoe, poinsettia and holly, which are poisonous to dogs; candles that could ignite a canine's wagging tail; and candy everywhere, including chocolate, which could kill your pet.

It's amazing that most of us survive these high-pressure holidays and then choose to do exactly the same thing a year later. So can you really blame your dog for absorbing all the holiday tension? Before the family sideshow descends on your house, anticipate the impact of all that impending action on your dog, especially if you're in the middle of a dog-training program that could be completely set back within only a few days of exposure to negative guests, human and canine.

Consider giving your pooch a holiday at a friend's place (as long as you trust that your friend will stick with your rules) or a good professional kennel. If that's not possible, don't neglect your dog's basic needs, even if you feel pressured to be the perfect holiday host with the two-legged members of the family. You can actually use the excuse that the dog needs a good walk twice a day to get some decompression time away from the chaos and maintain both your dog's balance and your own sanity.

You can't change the bad behaviour of other dog owners, but you can certainly enforce your own household rules. Tell your guests that human food is off-limits for your dog and that you don't allow *any* dogs on the furniture. Teach visiting kids the rules of dog engagement right away, and if they break those rules, it's your job to remove your dog to a quiet zone, ideally his own space or crate. Keeping your pooch in private quarters will also limit any dog-to-dog alpha scuffles. There's a good chance that your typically quiet and calm dog will at least bark at guest dogs when they break the rules, but if other dogs haven't been properly alpha trained and they've been humanized too much, things could escalate into a dog fight. Your dog might then take disciplinary matters into her own hands and to the extreme. And the last thing you need to celebrate the holidays is a trip to the ER.

Halloween is one of many holidays that are stressful for dogs, what with the doorbell ding-donging every minute and the parade of sugar-stoked kids arriving at the door moments later, screaming, "Trick or treat!" I always play music to muffle the commotion. For all seasonal and other celebrations, be considerate about how the accompanying upheavals might affect your dog, whether you stay home for the holidays or go away. Do your best to limit any potential stress so the entire family unit can share a relaxing and fun bonding experience during holidays.

Travelling with Dogs

If you're heading out of town on vacation, your decision to take your dog with you will depend on her personality. Does she have a lot of difficulty with airline travel or with kennels? If she's never flown before, anticipate her stress levels based on previous experiences, such as a trip to the vet. Does she get anxious in a crate or have separation anxiety when you're not around? If so, talk to your vet about sedation drugs to keep her mellow en route, but never play DIY doctor by using over-the-counter meds.

My dogs didn't have any problems with flying, car trips and hotels because they were well trained and they were exposed to a lot of variety from an early age. But some dogs are not so keen on being moved around. Even if your dog likes travelling as much as mine have, it's a good idea to prepare him for his trip a few days ahead of the departure date by giving him a lot of exercise. If he's travelling in cargo, do some crate training so he'll be less anxious and more apt to sleep through the voyage. Also, before you book your flight, do your homework by researching airlines' specific requirements, such as whether they allow dogs in the passenger cabin, the size limits for dog crates in the cabin and the cargo hold, and whether there are any blackout periods for pets. Some airlines have cargo pet restrictions during the cold winter and hot summer months, and there might also be restrictions on short-nosed breeds because they're sensitive to hot climates.

Don't feed your dog a meal just before a flight, but give her a small amount of water and make sure she has a bathroom break just before she's crated. Expect transportation delays and do your best to provide your dog with water and relief as soon as you arrive at your destination.

Some of my clients have literally become hostages in their own homes because they're too petrified to take their dog anywhere. But you can't succeed if you don't try, so once we've done basic training, I always encourage clients to try a new adventure with their pets.

One of my client couples was about to move back to Texas, but they had a home wrecker on their hands and envisioned her trashing the car in exactly the same way that she'd destroyed their home. But I got them into alpha position and showed them how to teach the dog to respect their human possessions and satisfy her basic dog needs. Then I gave them some survival tips for that long road trip to the Lone Star State. I told them to take the dog for a good rip before they first got on the road. I also encouraged them to break up the monotony en route by stopping at rest stops, parks and any interesting sights they passed, even "The World's Largest Ball of String," or whatever might fascinate both species At the very least, stopping to see the sights gives everyone an opportunity to stretch their legs and get the blood pumping. While the family was pit-stopped, I encouraged them to do brief spurts of agility training, umbilical and sit-stay to keep the dog attentive, along with hide-and-seek and playing fetch for mental stimulation.

I ran into that client a few years later when they were back in Calgary visiting relatives. The woman of the family said that road trip was the most enjoyable one the family had ever taken.

Recap: Home-Wrecking Hounds

Dogs act out for a variety of reasons, and their destructive habits are typically a reaction to human neglect. Though dogs need to be accountable for what they do, it's our job to establish and teach them the house rules. Here are my key pointers for minimalizing the potential for home wrecking:

* Establish and maintain your alpha position.
* Make sure you're providing your dog with adequate physical exercise and mental stimulation.
* Provide your dog with her own space for sleeping and relaxing and show respect for that space by keeping it neat and tidy and free of humans' belongings.
* Teach your dog what's off-limits and what's within bounds by interrupting any attempts to play with your possessions and by providing your dog with three toys.
* Play games with your dog to strengthen your bond and stave off boredom and anxiety.
* Be respectful of how household changes affect and stress out your dog.
* If a house rule has been broken, discipline your dog so he understands that the behaviour is unacceptable.

CHAPTER SEVEN

Coddled Canines

THE DANGERS OF HEAVY PETTING AND THE BEST METHODS FOR REWARDING YOUR DOG

MYTH: A clingy dog is simply a shy "Mama's kid," who prefers to be with you more than anyone else.

REALITY CHECK: Your dog is exhibiting depressed, anxious and fearful behaviours that can escalate to aggression and be very difficult to fix, especially in dogs separated from their four-legged mother before eight weeks of age.

A Perfect Storm

I picked Storm out of a crowd of dogs during a training session in Toronto. She was a beautiful jet-black German shepherd—the kind of dog that makes heads turn in admiration and would make even the most hardened criminals sweat. Yet this eight-year-old dog slunk around self-consciously like an old mule packing so much baggage that her shoulders were stooped over with the weight. It was obvious to me that Storm was a depressed, anxious, worn-down dog. I've seen enough of these animals over the years to know that this was a dog packing far too much of her owner's luggage.

I asked Storm's owner, Lesli, "What's wrong with this dog?" Lesli shrugged.

"This dog is sad," I said.

"I was a bit offended by that comment," admits Lesli. "But I didn't dismiss the idea. Then Brad said, 'Your dog's carrying a heavy emotional burden.' He really nailed it."

After the session wrapped up, I talked with Lesli about her recent past and the many things that had weighted this dog down to the point that she'd become so anxious and screwed up that on their rare outdoor jogs, she'd started lashing out at other dogs and people. Lesli admitted that Storm's aggressive behaviours started to develop after a series of very difficult events in Lesli's life caused her to withdraw from the world. That self-imposed exile naturally had a profoundly negative impact on Storm. Her basic dog needs weren't being met, and she was playing surrogate human partner—an impossible role for any dog.

To get both species out of the hole, I gave Lesli a five-point plan: alpha umbilical combined with no talking for two weeks (which was critical, since Lesli tended to baby-talk to Storm); turfing Storm from Lesli's bed and all the human furniture; hide-and-seek games to both stimulate Storm's mind and give the two an opportunity to let loose and have fun; patience training so Storm could learn that it was okay to be alone; and most importantly, motivating Lesli to appreciate that her dog couldn't possible fulfill all of her human needs. Luckily, Lesli got that message immediately and dog training

was actually a catalyst for getting her own life back on track—
a life that was worth sharing with her awesome dog.

I'll get to the details of these exercises soon, but first let
me clarify that I don't pretend to be a psychic or a mind
reader. I've met plenty of dogs whose owners have heaped
so much of their own emotional baggage onto their dogs'
backs that the dog had no choice but to take leadership. So
it was not too difficult to see, simply from observation, that
Storm was carrying too much emotional burden.

In an unhealthy situation like that, dogs will become code-
pendent emotional sherpas who can't stand being alone and
have huge insecurity issues. Dogs are social animals, but like
us, they should also be able to enjoy, or at least tolerate, spending time on their own. Dogs separated from their mothers
before eight weeks of age often have separation anxiety, and
it can be really tough to help those animals become comfortable and relaxed on their own. Many times, the problem
can be curbed, but I have worked with hundreds of dogs who
were removed from the litter too early, and some of them
can never be fixed.

Even if a pup has joined her human family after the appropriate time with her dog mom, dog owners often *create* these
separation anxiety issues by overcoddling their dogs and
taking the "man's best friend" idea to the extreme. Sometimes
the human prefers a dog's company to that of anybody else,
and they project their own personality onto their pet, at the
expense of the dog. I know plenty of well-adjusted canines
who prefer human company to dog company, and not all dogs
are party animals. Some dogs are also shy, but if they're shy to
the point of not being able to function in the world without
lapsing into hysterics or lashing out, they will obviously

become a problem dog. People need to come to terms with the fact that a clingy dog who runs and hides every time they see their own shadow, or becomes territorially aggressive is dysfunctional and anxious and could be downright deadly. I can only determine what's really going on with this type of dog by working with the dog and finding out whether his personality and makeup play a part or whether that animal has become manipulative either because the owner has been negligent with training or has caved in and given up on training. The problem may also lie in the fact that the owner has neglected to foster the dog's confidence and self-esteem. Doing exercises like agility training, which gives the dog confidence, is absolutely critical to helping an insecure canine get on the right path. The dog also needs to be taught that it's okay to be alone. If she throws a scary tantrum every time you leave the room, start with leaving her alone for a minute and build it up. Then gradually start introducing her to new settings to test the threshold.

In order to have any success, it's vital to have a lot of patience when you're working with a dog who has separation anxiety. It can take months of hard work to build up a dog's self-esteem and independence, and there's no such thing as a one-size-fits-all training method. But there are many ways to help that dog become a balanced, functioning member of society.

Red Flags for Separation Anxiety

Many of my dog clients came to their owners packing separation issues. So we have to look back at the dog's history to figure out how long he's been dysfunctional. If you got the dog from the breeder before the age of eight weeks, there's a good chance he'll be in danger of developing anxiety issues. You might not know the specifics of your dog's past, but as I'll discuss in more detail in Chapter 9, it's a buyer-beware market. Prospective dog owners therefore need to educate themselves about the practices of breeders, pet shops and shelters. It's also really important to glean as much as possible about the dog's history from the breeder, shelter or previous owner when you first get the dog.

Dogs often develop separation anxiety because their owners have neglected their basic dog needs. These pets will then engage in the negative behaviours I've already discussed, including assuming the alpha role, barking at everything that moves, being rude or fearful among other dogs and trashing the home when the owners are out. But I'll highlight specific separation anxiety behaviours here so you can assess whether your dog needs separation anxiety training:

* When you leave your home, your dog destroys or trashes his crate, the laundry room or any other area that you've designated as his chill-out zone.
* He attempts to chew through doors or dig at the floor under closed doors.
* She gets into excessive whining, barking or shivering as soon as you leave home or whenever you leave her side.
* She exhibits fear-based aggressive tendencies around other dogs and people—including deep growling, baring teeth, lowering her head, compressing her neck, assuming any self-protective body language and lashing out when people or other dogs approach.
* He demonstrates excessively shy behaviour around other dogs and people, such as hiding behind your legs, diving under a table or chair or bolting away.

These negative behaviours are unacceptable, and your dog needs to learn that she's accountable for them. But they often go hand-in-hand with negative human behaviours, so it's imperative that you assess and correct your own traits and actions too. Generally speaking, people with dogs who develop separation anxiety set few to no rules of dog conduct. Either that or they're fickle about those rules, which compounds the issues by confusing the dog. Owners may also foster a dog's insecurities because of their own unique subset of negative human traits and behaviours—crippling and sometimes completely disabling a dog's many great strengths. Instead of respecting and drawing on those wonderful dog traits and allowing him to develop his own unique personality, many owners of dogs with separation anxiety saddle them with these issues by behaving in a variety of different and often conflicting ways. Here's a list of some of those negative human actions:

* Constantly petting, carrying and/or talking to the dog.
* Bonding with the dog by cuddling on the couch instead of providing outdoor exercise and mental stimulation.
* Isolating the dog from other people and dogs.
* Using the dog as a surrogate human partner, friend or family member.
* Encouraging the dog's insecurities by tolerating and making excuses for negative behaviours like whining, barking or aggression.
* Showering the dog with toys, props and unhealthy food treats.
* Dressing the dog up like a cute little doll.
* Ignoring the dog's *doggy* needs.

In order to start curbing your dog's separation anxiety, you have to be willing to take a good look at how your own behaviours negatively affect your dog. And you need to commit to a consistent training program that busts these learned behaviours in both species.

Lap Dogs

One thing that slays me is the overcoddling behaviour of some dog owners who treat their dogs like babies, carrying them everywhere, or use them as comfort blankets and insist on keeping their dogs on their laps and in their beds—you know who you are!

I've met dogs who've never touched the ground because they've been carried *everywhere*. These dogs don't understand the world the way a normal dog should. They've been denied the fulfillment of their hard-wired needs to pick up scents, textures, sounds and sights from the ground. They're literally ungrounded. You know what this coddled dog will do almost any time she's given a chance? She'll lash out— often at her owner's face when they're cheek-to-jaw, but the dog could try to attack any encroaching hand or body part. Why? The dog's innate needs—to be close to the ground as much as possible, to have all her doggy needs satisfied, including time to be free and independent—have been suppressed for so long that eventually, she won't be able to take it anymore and she'll strike out.

People need to understand that overcoddling on the part of humans can have deadly consequences. People will say, "Oh, Rex is such a mama's boy," but most of the time, the person is projecting their own human characteristics and self-indulgences onto the dog, while the dog's needs aren't being met. A coddled dog has low self-esteem and high anxiety levels and is simply and heartbreakingly a broken dog. We must quit pouring excessive amounts of human affection and other emotions onto animals.

It's a big challenge to treat dogs with anxiety disorders because so much of the work involves training the client to change. As I've said before, dogs usually take really well to training; it's the people who are tough to manage. It's not just about having the time, energy, patience and dedication to commit to a training program; it's also about breaking your own habits and getting rid of your own addictions, fears and anxieties. This can be particularly difficult for the many people who are dealing with tough times, such as grieving the death of a loved one or going through a divorce.

The situation was like this for Lesli, the owner of the jet-black German shepherd introduced at the beginning of this chapter. She had to commit to training Storm after her own life had fallen to pieces.

Storm: Only the Lonely

Storm had no boundaries in her life. The big, beautiful, seventy-five-pound dog was allowed on the furniture and encouraged to cuddle with Lesli on the couch, and she slept in her owner's bed. Then, when Lesli's personal life turned upside down, Lesli did what a number of my clients do when the going gets tough: she started leaning even more heavily on her dog to fulfill her own emotional needs.

"Storm started showing aggression to other dogs when she was about seven years old," remembers Lesli. "She only did it occasionally, so I didn't think much of it at the time. Mostly, she was still a great dog and we had no problems at the dog park. Then she started getting worked up whenever she saw a rollerblader, a skateboarder or anything else on wheels. After a while, even a bus or a jogger would set her off. One day, the dog walker left a note: 'Storm was bad. We'll talk soon.' It turned out she'd turned on a dog that she'd been walked with for two years. I started to wonder, Who was this dog?

"At that point, I thought that maybe she was just stressed because I'd been travelling a lot with work and a crazy schedule. A few months later, this past May, my whole life turned upside down. I got pregnant and my boyfriend left. It was devastating for me and for Storm; she really loved my ex. I'd always been really affectionate with Storm, talking to her a lot, saying, 'How was your day, Boo Boo?' But now I was pretty much mauling the poor thing. I was also really sick with the pregnancy and then I miscarried. I withdrew and started hiding out at home, avoiding friends. Storm was the only one I felt safe with. I put all of my emotional and psychological needs on her. I felt like crap and my self-esteem was in the toilet.

"One day, I was walking Storm and she lunged after a jogger. She didn't break skin, but it was a scary scene. I contacted an animal behaviourist who used treats to make Storm cooperate. I spent a bunch of money to get a Band-Aid effect. The treat training didn't help at all. I started getting much more paranoid when we went out for walks and met other dogs, and I guess I started taking her out less to avoid these problems."

Lesli was doing some Internet research about canine aggression when she came across my site, listing a seminar in Toronto. Like so many of my clients, she felt this was a last resort.

"After Brad and I talked, we set up a training plan," says Lesli. "Number one was to kick Storm out of my bed and off all the furniture. Also no talking for two weeks, umbilical training, outdoor agility training, and playing hide-and-seek in the house. I was ready to commit to those things. I also decided to get my own counselling to lighten the emotional load I'd been dumping on Storm.

"I didn't get much sleep those first few nights, and Storm was pretty shocked by the new rules. She cried and whined. It was really tough, but I knew I needed to be consistent. It took about ten to fourteen days before she stopped trying to jump up on all the furniture, but with the no talking rule and the umbilical, I saw immediate positive changes: she was more relaxed but also more attentive to my authority. A lot of the time, I had to fake confidence around her because I still had my own self-esteem issues. But within days on umbilical, she was walking right beside me. It actually helped boost my confidence, too, and her insecurities also decreased with hide-and-seek, which she loved doing. Also the agility training, running around trees, over picnic tables and on the playground ramps. We were really a team, building up our confidence together.

"It's been four weeks now since I started doing the training program. The other day, she walked right by a Westie without barking and wasn't fazed at all by a leaf blower in the park, which would have set her off in the past. I don't even have to hold the leash at the dog park; I still keep her leash on, so that if a greeting goes south, I can stand on the leash. I realize we're not out of the woods yet. Storm is an intelligent dog, so she tests me sometimes.

"To be honest, it's often me hitting my own walls. I had a couple of bad days last week. One night, I even collapsed on the couch and started to cry. Storm came up to me and tried to lick my tears. But she didn't try to get on the couch, and even though I felt so down, I didn't cave and start leaning on her for affection; I didn't put the pressure on her. That means I no longer use her as an excuse to hide out on a Friday night. In the past I would have said I felt guilty leaving her alone, but it was really because of my issues of trust and loneliness. I find myself saying, 'Yes' more to going out with friends and trying new things.

"The funny thing is that Storm has always been curious about everything in life, and now that she's confident, relaxed and free to be a dog, she's able to show me what a goofy and smart dog she really is. I now realize that she has a completely different set of needs. I understand that the ultimate goal is for both of us to find the balance."

INSECURE DOGS

*D*ogs with separation anxiety are more likely to bark, engage in destructive behaviours and have elimination problems, say researchers at the Veterinary Technology Program in Pennsylvania.[35] Single people are also 2.5 times more likely to have dogs with this disorder, based on studies carried out at Tufts University's School of Veterinary Medicine.[36] These anxious dogs were more likely to have "departure cue anxiety" and to engage in "excessive greeting." Another study, based in Tokyo, found that dogs with separation anxiety are more often given only verbal discipline when they misbehave.[37]

Life Support

I've seen it happen time after time: once a person dedicates themselves to turning their own lives around and stops leaning on the dog to fulfill human needs that the pet can't possibly meet, the very act of dog training becomes a catalyst for getting their own lives back on track. This is especially true for people who humanize and coddle their dogs to fill a void in their own lives. With dedicated individuals, training the dog to become comfortable in her own fur sets off a chain reaction of positive forces in the dog owner's life. Dogs can bring back the heartbeat and the pulse so people are not just willing and able to get back on their own two feet; they're energized and excited about sharing the gifts of life with their dogs.

Correcting Separation Anxiety with Patience Training

Clingy dogs and dogs with separation anxiety hate to be alone. They've become so dependent on their owners that they can't stand being apart from them. As I've already described, humans can play a major role in *creating* these issues, and it's essential for us to train ourselves out of these negative human behaviours. All the training methods I suggested for Lesli were foundations for building up both species' confidence levels, all of which curbed Storm's anxieties and insecurities. Patience training goes a step further in teaching a dog how to get along on her own by making it clear that control-freak behaviour is unacceptable.

If your dog goes ballistic every time you start to leave the house, try the following patience training exercise:

* Walk out the front door.

* As soon as your dog starts to chirp, bark or whine, open the door again and say, "No noise" in a firm voice.
* Re-exit and wait to see whether she starts to whine or bark again.
* If she starts whining or barking, repeat the no noise command and leave again.
* Did she freak out again? Repeat the no noise command and leave.
* Wait outside the front door for up to ten minutes.
* If your dog acts out at any point during this period, consider returning and giving her a leash correction. Then leave again.
* You might have to do this exercise many times before your dog learns that it's okay to be alone.
* Your dog might also engage in all sorts of manipulation tactics meant to make you cave in—but don't do it. If you do, you'll have to start back at square one, and that could damage your dog even more.

Whatever you do, don't reward the dog for good behaviour with high-pitched verbal praise or with a lot of human physical affection. In fact, with overcoddled dogs, no verbal commands or verbal praise should be used for at least two weeks, other than the ones used during training exercises. In other words, this process is like the alpha training process. Consistency is always key with dog-human relations, and it's downright critical with separation anxiety dogs.

It's also a great idea to do this kind of patience training at the dog park, so that you're mixing up your pooch's basic doggy needs with training. Here's how to do it:

* First go for a good romp and play together for a while.
* Find a tree and request that your dog stay. With clingy dogs who are in little danger of bolting, keep the dog leashed up but drop the leash to the ground so you can stand on it if the dog does bolt. For dogs with aggressive tendencies or dogs who don't know how to go off-leash, use a twenty- or thirty-foot (six- to nine-metre) leash.
* Start walking away from your dog with your body squarely facing her Since you'll be walking backwards, check the terrain ahead of time to make sure you don't trip or bump into anything.
* Count the seconds as you move way.
* If your dog runs to you, put her back in a stay and start the process again.
* Continue the process until you have built up to the point that your dog can stay long enough for you to walk about twenty or thirty paces away.
* Give your dog a good chest scrunch and play for a while.
* The next time you go to the park, notch up the distance between you and the dog, ideally until you are out of each other's field of vision.
* Do a three-minute stay.
* Return and praise your dog.
* Repeat the same exercise, gradually increasing the distance until your dog can stay for ten minutes.
* Keep practising this exercise whenever you go to the park, so you know your dog can maintain a ten-minute stay.

* Start mixing hide-and-seek in with the training. Unlike the case in the hide-and-seek exercises described in Chapter 6, don't hide your dog's toys; instead, hide yourself. That way, your dog will begin to build up confidence while you're out of sight.
* When you're ready to be found, call out, "Come" and wait for your dog to find you.
* Don't let your dog pounce on you. If she tries to do that, interrupt her just as her paws leave the ground but put some enthusiasm in your tone and give your dog a good chest scrunch.

Do the same patience training while grabbing a coffee at a café. Leash your dog up outside and monitor his behaviour while you're inside. Is he shivering even though it's not cold outside? Is he whimpering or barking? chewing on the leash or acting anxiously in any way? If so, you still have more patience training to do.

Months of training are sometimes needed before a dog becomes functional on her own, but many people have too short a supply of their own patience to patience-train their dogs.

If your anxious, insecure dog is a home wrecker, consider putting her in her crate when you go out. If you're in a nine-to-five job during the crate phase, also consider coming home at lunchtime to give the dog some freedom. Or if that's not possible, think about hiring a dog walker to come over at midday, at least for a few months, to let your dog out for some fresh air. Whether you choose to do that or not, make sure that when you come home, you take your dog out and also play good stimulation games like hide-and-seek.

Unfortunately, it's not possible to fix every dog with separation anxiety, particularly dogs removed from the litter too early. If you've put the time and effort into training your dog and also meeting his needs but he is still too difficult to handle, particularly if he bites someone, you might have to consider euthanizing the dog. As an alternative, you might be able to send the dog to a ranch where there's a lot of space and not much human contact that would put others in danger. But if you do know of a place like that, be completely honest about the dog's issues so you're not putting anyone else in danger.

With hard work, consistency, commitment to human lifestyle changes and a whole heap of patience, most dogs with separation anxiety will eventually be able to stand on their own four paws. The perfect storm will calm eventually, with all parties respecting and celebrating each other's unique needs and personalities.

CANINE COMPULSIVE DISORDER

Dogs with canine compulsive disorder (CCD) have been effectively treated with anti-anxiety drugs, but researchers at the Ontario Agricultural College found that the meds weren't curative and suggested that non-drug-based behaviour modification programs were likely necessary for managing CCD.[38]

Obsessive-Compulsive Dogs

I've met some dogs who've been so starved of physical and mental stimulation that they've become obsessive-compulsive, fixating on a specific possession or small animals or self-mutilating. It breaks my heart to see a dog become so desperate that she hurts herself (chewing on her own paw or licking herself until she bleeds), becomes possession-obsessed or fixates on every squirrel in the backyard. Obsessive-compulsive disorders have only recently become the subject of study among animal behaviourists. Dogs with this problem will take normal behaviours to the extreme—grooming, running and pacing, spinning around, tail chasing, fixating on light or shadows (even their own shadows) and interacting obsessively with other animals (which can result in predatory behaviours). Some dogs will obsess over an object, licking it all the time.

Researchers are doing investigations to find out why dogs develop canine compulsive disorder, but it's a tricky one to diagnose. So far, hunting and working breeds appear to be the most susceptible, and maybe there's a genetic component, but my dogs Dez and Max and so many other working breeds I've known have never had these kinds of issues. I suspect that some dogs develop the disorder due to a combination of boredom, too much human stress in their lives and neglect of their doggy needs. However, there may be physical reasons for the problem. If your dog is hurting himself or exhibiting aggressive behaviours, get to the vet immediately. It's quite possible that a virus or other physical problem may be causing these behavioural issues. Be on the lookout for abnormal behaviours as soon as you notice them and make sure your dog's needs are met.

Be careful not to rush to assume that your dog has a genetic disorder before you've addressed the potential human causes of doggy neglect. Too many people blame genes and breed when, in fact, their own behaviours have turned normal doggy behaviours into serious obsessive problems. Once that happens, your dog becomes hostage to that negative fixation, which suffocates all her unique characteristics. Please do your best to prevent that from happening. Give your dog the wonderful human gift of caring, respectful guidance, so she'll be able to give her individual doggy gifts to you.

ACTIVITY-IMPULSIVITY

*J*uvenile dogs had higher "activity-impulsivity" and "inattention" scores in a poll of dog owners conducted by researchers at the Family Dog Project in Budapest, who were looking at attention-deficit disorder. Small dogs also had higher "activity-impulsivity" scores than larger dogs. But dogs who'd received training had lower inattention scores than untrained dogs.[39]

Doggy Attention Deficit

Recently, I've been meeting more and more dogs who've been diagnosed with psychiatric labels like ADHD (attention deficit hyperactivity disorder). I'm meeting more kids tagged with the ADHD label, too, but I'll leave that topic to the child psychologists. I can't speak for every dog categorized in this way, and the diagnosis may be accurate in some cases.

In-breeding issues might play a role in behaviour problems and removing a puppy from the litter before eight weeks of age will definitely set them up for a whole bag of negative issues. However, many of the medicated dogs I've met weren't even given a crack at learning and cultivating their skills, and some were still puppies! Aren't puppies typically wired for sound and always cranked to play and explore? Isn't that one of the things we love about a puppy? Of course, they need to learn the rules of behaviour, but it's our human duty to allow them the time and space to be puppies, which means providing them with a lot of physical and mental stimulation and letting them explore the world around them.

Many of my clients who've come to me with medicated dogs were advised by trainers who didn't have proper training skills. The trainer had advised the vet to medicate, and the vet had too much blind faith in the trainer's advice. Drugs are used far too often as a quick-fix, which masks the root problem. I've seen too many doped-up dogs out there. Drugs undermine the intelligence, energy and beauty of those animals. They create cobwebs of confusion and chaos and make effective dog training much more difficult.

One of my client dogs was a ten-month-old pup who'd been diagnosed as "hyperactive" by a previous trainer. When I met him at his home, he was certainly buzzing, jumping up at me and trying to engage me to play. My client wasn't home yet, so I talked to her daughter for a while and assessed the dog. Under all that energy, I saw a dog that simply needed some basic rules and skills that would draw out his potential. When his mom came home, she said, "Oh, he's so hyperactive," then turned to the daughter and said, "Didn't you give him his meds today?"

For puppies, life is a celebration. It's certainly our job to balance the party with rules and boundaries just as mother dogs teach their pups behaviour skills. It's also our job to educate dogs so they can get along in *our* world. And just like pup moms, we need to provide discipline if a puppy breaks the rules.

So, somehow, drugs are supposed to replace all of that? or act as a Band-Aid that will magically keep the dog from falling apart? In my view, they don't do any of that. They only stifle the dog's energy and trick the dog into appearing calm. This masks both their potential and negative emotions like aggression. And since these drugs can actually cause negative side effects in humans,[40] why assume that they wouldn't have negative side effects for your dog?

All dogs should be given a good crack at being trained before their owners even think about giving them drugs. In the case of the "hyper" puppy that I just described, through consistent training, I was able to show this family some basic steps that helped calm the dog and tune his attention to them. My client stopped dosing the dog with drugs and committed herself to learning how to foster a well-behaved dog. But most importantly, she and the entire family committed themselves to meeting the dog's needs for a lot of physical exercise and stimulation and a social life worth celebrating. This was a great, outgoing, energetic and smart family. They needed to see that their dog yearned for just as much variety and balance, so he could share in the wealth and give back his own riches.

Retail Therapy: Not for the Dogs

One of the first things I do with clients is snoop around their home to find out what kinds of collars, leashes, toys, treats and other doggy props they have. In far too many cases, they have too much of everything, and few of those props are effective. Some are downright draconian, like pinch collars and electrical bark collars. Some of my clients' dogs have bigger and more expensive wardrobes and more deluxe toys than their parents. I often have to dig beneath all that junk to figure out what's really going on.

Some of these clients are grieving a loss, such as the death of a loved one. They're pouring all that grief into retail dog therapy. Some clients have low self-esteem and feel they have to buy everybody's love, dog included. Others simply think that because there are so many big box outlets and designer dog boutiques everywhere, crammed with aisle upon aisle of stuff, there must be a need for all of it. The truth is that the majority of those things are useless. It absolutely infuriates me that our society manufactures so much junk and manipulates us into believing that we need to spend a whole bunch of money on lifestyle products for our dogs: ridiculous clothing, thousand-dollar beds, gourmet food—and all of it in overabundance.

People who dog-shop till they drop desperately need to get a *life* instead of falling into the trap of believing they need to somehow *buy* a lifestyle. In my view, more is more when you spend your hard-earned recreational *time* bonding with your family. Too often we're guilted into buying consumer items to serve as surrogates for good old-fashioned fun and entertainment. I'm not about to tell you how to spend your money on yourself and your human family, but I think our throwaway culture sends really unhealthy messages to younger generations. What's the crime in a well-balanced life? Get out of the store and into the park!

Less is especially more in the dog's view when it comes to props. Dogs don't give a darn about the fancy labels, but they can sure tell the difference between an itchy little sweater with an expensive label and a good outdoor rip. Dogs want your time and your attention in a variety of stimulating environments. They don't want useless stuff.

Having too many props actually causes too much confusion in a dog's life, and it encourages bad doggy behaviours. People will say, "But look how many toys there are for kids!" That sentiment—especially among people who overcoddle their dogs and treat them like babies—usually includes the idea that we need the same for dogs. I'd argue that kids also have too many toys, but I'll leave that topic to the child psychologists too. But for dogs, having a lot of toys creates problems, especially if they live with kids. In that case, they'll have trouble figuring out which toys are off limits. Don't get me wrong, a good collar and leash are essential. So are a few toys because they help develop important physical and cognitive skills, as well as providing excellent opportunities for bonding and play. But you don't need to spend a fortune at pet stores on these supplies. You can often find better, more durable and much less expensive items at hardware stores and butcher shops and by making use of old towels, T-shirts and socks.

At the end of this chapter, I'll discuss products that are essential for dogs to maintain health and fitness. But please remember that props should be used not as "ends in themselves" but as complements to other forms of physical and mental stimulation, including good exercise, agility training and fun games like hide-and-seek. Whether you live in a tiny urban apartment or a huge house with a backyard, you can avoid the toy trap (which isn't eco-friendly anyway) by making use of all sorts of things in your immediate environment. Benches, stairs, logs and simple playground equipment—all of these can be used to enrich your bonding time with your dog.

Pimping the Pooch

Ironically, spoiling dogs with so many possessions actually causes negative behaviours when they're used as a substitute for spending real quality time with your pet. And if your dog is neglected (even though surrounded by baubles and toys), he'll seek restitution by targeting *your* possessions. I met a pimped pooch recently in the lineup at Starbucks. The dog was pinned up to his owner's chest like a yappy piece of lapel jewellery. The owner recognized me from my TV show and started filling me in about how her "naughty like baby boy" was always peeing in the house. As she fed him biscotti dunked in mocha latte to keep his mouth busy, she said she was considering ditching him if it continued. I asked about their daily rituals, and it turned out that her dog's feet rarely ever touched ground. But when they did, she expected he'd get right down to business and pee. I gave her the usual drill about a dog's basic needs. She gave me a response that I hear so often: "He doesn't know he's a dog. He thinks he's a person." "Oh, well, in that case," I said, "no wonder you want to get rid of him. If your husband peed on the toilet seat, you'd get rid of him too, right?" "Oh Brad, don't be crazy," said she. Oh, yeah? Who's the one with the Hells Doggy in a studded leather motorcycle jacket and matching leather chaps?

Notice the mixed messages this woman was sending out to her dog? On the one hand, she was humanizing him to the extreme, dressing him up, feeding him human food, carrying him around all the time and cuddling him like an infant. But on other hand, she was ready to turn him in like last year's fad designer bag. I completely agree that peeing all over the place is unacceptable behaviour, but as are the cases of so many of my pimped pooch clients, this woman had likely been offered no structured training program. And her dog, by being forced to play surrogate human and cutesie dog all rolled into one, what choice did he have but to act out?

DOGGY AFFLUENZA

U.S. dog owners spend over $100 billion annually on their 74.8 million dogs according to a survey by the American Pet Products Manufacturers Association.[41] On the other side of the Atlantic, 43 per cent of dog owners polled in The Netherlands said that their dogs had one or more behaviour problems, and dissatisfaction with dogs' negative issues increased with higher-income dog owners.[42]

The Ideal Ways to Praise and Reward Your Dog

Praise is extremely important for dogs. It gives them a clear understanding of what we appreciate and expect from them in the same way that discipline teaches them how to avoid negative behaviours. The best way to acknowledge that your dog is phenomenal is to meet her basic needs. I'm probably sounding like a broken record at this point, but this is the critical factor, the glue of interspecies bonding. And by being the household alpha and providing your dog with adequate exercise and mental stimulation, you will be feeding your dog a steady diet of praise and respect. Another great way to reward your pooch is to let him show you what he can do. That means giving your dog time off-leash so he has some freedom to be a dog.

Wild dogs show their affection for each other through play, so you can be an awesome surrogate dog partner by taking your canine companion for a good rip outside or getting down on the floor and engaging your dog with fun games. I make a game out of simple daily situations. For example, when I leave my dog Rudy in the car while I run an errand, I say, "Rudy, watch the car, buddy." I don't expect that Rudy will actually fend off burglars, but I think it makes him feel useful. Then, when I come back, I'll give him a good scrunch on the chest, and he'll know he did something right simply by being a patient, relaxed, well-behaved dog.

Of course, physical touch is not off-limits, but people often get carried away with petting their pooch, especially while they're vegging with the dog on the lap. It becomes a ritualized activity, and sometimes they're not even conscious that they're doing it. By now I'm really hoping you've made a pact with yourself to stop with the lap dog thing. Get down on ground level to pet your dog.

Many people pet their dogs on the shoulder, the side and the stomach, but in my opinion, the best spot is the chest area. Once your dog has earned some praise, give her a slow, gentle chest massage with the tips of your fingers. Massaging your dog is a great way to bond, and it also helps you get to know your dog's body. Then, if you discover any lumps or abnormalities, you'll know that she needs to see a vet. And if your dog has become comfortable with in-house massages, she probably won't freak when the vet examines her. While you're massaging the dog, keep your mouth zipped so she can truly relax, just the way a good massage therapist doesn't rattle away at you.

The True Pampered Pooch

Dogs don't feel loved because they sleep in our beds, serve as breast warmers, endure high-pitched baby talk or loaf on the couch all night instead of going for a good outdoor rip. A truly caring dog owner realizes that a dog is a dog and that these activities humanize the dog to their disadvantage. People often say that they'd like to come back in a next life as their pet dog (meaning that they'd then be taken care of very well). I suspect that some of them are in utter denial that the dog's not getting anything she needs *as a dog*. Many dogs are alone all day, and a secure dog will be sleeping for much of that time, but I doubt any of them would be dreaming of a big night sitting on the couch eating popcorn and staring at weird, flickering images on a screen.

If I did have to be reincarnated right now as any one living dog I know, it would be as Rocky, the awesome Australian shepherd I talked about in Chapter 4. That dog has a daytimer jam-packed with good times. On weekends, he gets two nice, long outdoor adventures with Steve and Peggy. They take him to parks along the river so he can swim, hunt in the bushes and socialize with other dogs. They trust Rocky to have some alone time, and he's free to go off-leash, periodically checking back in with his parents. They know that training is an ongoing process that also helps keep Rocky stimulated mentally, so they'll throw some stop, stay or come commands into the mix. These training games satisfy Rocky's working dog needs, and that's the best method of rewarding praise. Then they go grab a latte and spend some time chilling and mixing with other people and dogs before heading home.

During the week, Rocky used to come to daycare to hang out with Dez, Max and the other dogs. And once he was well trained, he worked as one of my helper dogs, doing umbilical training and helping teach dogs proper dog etiquette. It gave me such a kick to see this once totally messed up canine helping other dogs find the way.

Now that I've moved away, Chantal, one of my Certified Educator Trainers (CETs) comes over to take Rocky for walks with a posse of other dogs, and in the evenings, Steve takes him out for another rip. I make a point of seeing the family whenever I can. They're like extended family to me now that Rocky's been a part of my life for so long, and I can't imagine them without Rocky. They really have it all now that they get the most out of each other.

Essential Dog Products

Dogs do need a few essential products to maintain good mental and physical health. As I pointed out in the previous chapter, they need a good bed or another comfortable space for sleeping and chilling out, and as I'll discuss below, they also need three good toys, healthy dog food and some basic grooming products.

Pet Shop Toys

Toys are not only an important tool for bonding and engaging your dog in play and mental stimulation games; they also help him improve his motor skills and coordination of his mouth and paws so he can learn to clasp and release objects, become more dexterous in other ways, too, and develop important interactive skills. Playing will improve your dog's confidence, and it gives you a great opportunity for affection, praise and stress-busting fun. By playing a variety of games like fetch, chase, hide-and-seek and tug, you can help your dog become well rounded, and these are some of the most fun and positive ways to refresh the rules of engagement.

When you play with your dog, he's paying attention to you in the most positive way and you're doing the same. So when your dog bounds up and lays one of his favourite toys in front of you, think of it as a unique gift: he's inviting you to play and bond with him. Don't betray that gift by ignoring your dog. If you don't have the time to play right then, be sure to acknowledge your dog immediately anyway. Dogs, like people, will process your inattention as rejection and be less likely to try to engage you in the future. That would be a shame, so don't dismiss your dog's need to play and bond. Give him a chest rub and say, "Later, dog" and mean it—ideally within twenty-four hours. And then, don't wait for your pooch to come to you again. Instead, take the initiative by getting the toy he set down in front of you and saying, "Now I'm ready. Let's play."

As I said earlier, your dog needs only three toys. Any more than that will make it tougher for her to discern between her own possessions and yours. Look for a variety of toys that your individual dog gravitates toward and that can be used for different types of play: a rope toy for tug, a rubber ball or a *soft* Frisbee for playing fetch and a squeaky or furry toy for playing hide-and-seek and other mental stimulation games (but make sure there are no plastic buttons on the toy that your dog might swallow. (Note that hard Frisbees must not be used, since they could damage your dog's teeth or nose.) Also make sure your dog has something to gnaw on, such as a toy called Kong, or get a real meat or buffalo bone from the butcher shop that has a lot of marrow. (Bones are also great for tooth cleaning and will save you a lot of money on dental bills.)

Follow your dog's nose when it comes to toys. Take her to the pet store, put a variety of different toys on the ground and relax the leash or let go of it so your dog has some freedom to test out the goods. Take a few steps back and avoid making eye contact with your dog. That way, when she's ready to pick a toy, she can use her eyes as pointers.

Some toys are unsafe. Tennis balls, for instance, can wreak havoc because they're like nail files, and they'll wear down doggy teeth. Wood sticks and rawhide bones can also be dangerous: dogs can ingest bark that might contain dangerous pesticides, and rawhide will swell over time, break off and get lodged in your dog's digestive tract. Hard Frisbees are also a bad idea because, as mentioned before, they damage teeth and could break a dog's schnozz.

A Balanced Dog Diet

Never feed your puppy, or any dog, human food. Not only does this foster bad behaviours like cruising counters and food-related aggressions, but some of the foods we find delectable are far too high in fat for our dogs to digest and some are actually poisonous and lethal to them—including mushrooms, grapes and even a small amount of chocolate. (Check with your local SPCA for a complete list.)

I use dry dog food or a raw dog food because they're better for dogs' teeth. They also typically have better ingredients than many of the wet, canned foods, which contain too much water and not enough protein and nutrients. I always alternate flavours so the dogs don't get bored. When the bag of chicken and rice kibble is empty, I move on to a bag of lamb and rice. As the saying goes, variety is the spice of life.

DOG OBESITY

*T*he majority of dog owners reported that their dogs were overweight or obese according to a large Australia/U.S. study done in 2006.[43] But of the owners of the 635 dogs in the survey, only three said the dog's weight was a health problem. Another study, from the U.S., found that 40 per cent of dogs between the ages of five and ten were overweight or obese.[44]

The Essential Doggy Grooming Kit

Grooming is a necessary daily activity for all dogs. Some breeds are meticulous with hygiene and clean themselves many times a day, while other breeds are less detail oriented. Wild dogs also clean each other, and those of us who have more than two household dogs have seen this activity in action. The scope and nature of a canine's self-grooming will also depend on her level of outdoor activity, so it's best to follow your dog's cue. After a good outdoor escapade, watch your dog clean herself and take note of how long she spends on personal hygiene. All the same, a dog can't do everything herself, and while domestic dogs might get less dirty than wild dogs, they might also need more assistance from us human caregivers with things like grooming and bathing. To maintain your dog's health and hygiene, you will need a grooming brush, a pair of scissors to get rid of matted hair, a shampoo and conditioner and a toothbrush and toothpaste.

A good grooming brush will have firm bristles. With long-haired dogs, you'll need long-toothed bristles—at least a half-inch long (a bit more than half a centimetre). For shorthaired coats, look for short bristles. Brush your dog in four directions: east, west, north and south. Place your brush in the middle of the spine and brush right around to the dog's underbelly. Then reverse the brush direction back up toward the dog's spine. Next, start brushing from the hindquarters and work toward the dog's head and chest, using short strokes. Repeat the process from the head back down to the hindquarters and then do the same thing on the opposite side of the dog.

You shouldn't have to clip your dog's nails. If they grow too long, that means the dog's not getting enough outdoor exercise, so start attending to those needs pronto. In winter months, you might have to get the dog's nails clipped by a pro, but I've never had to do this with my dogs during any of the long, cold Canadian winters we've been through. Even if nail cutting shouldn't likely be needed, it's a good idea to inspect your dog's paws periodically for cuts and abrasions. Outdoor dogs will have thicker and more resilient paw pads than indoor dogs, so be extra vigilant if you take an indoor dog on a big romp, especially around concrete or rocky surfaces and especially during the summer months, when surfaces heat up.

You'll need scissors for cutting out large mats in your canine companion's fur. These form when shed hair mixes with the new hair. If you don't cut out these mats, they'll start to grow and pull at your dog's skin. By removing them, you'll also help your dog stay cool, but that doesn't mean you should leave the mats there when the weather is cold. Mats are painful for a dog at any time of year.

Bathtime should happen every few months. Look for organic, all-natural products that won't irritate your pooch's skin. If you're not sure what products suit your dog's breed, talk to a professional groomer about the best ones for your specific dog. Also use bathtime to massage your pet's body. She'll enjoy the rub, and massaging will also give you time to check for cuts, mats or internal lumps that could indicate a health problem. Be on the lookout for ticks and bugs that might get into your dog's ears. Smell the dog's ears periodically, and if they smell pungent, take the dog to a vet.

Caring for your dog's teeth is also very important because dogs can actually become sick if their teeth aren't properly maintained. Some dogs are born with hard enamel. That was the case with my Dez, who had brilliant white teeth her entire life. Max, on the other hand, had super-soft teeth, so gnawing on real beef bones with a lot of marrow helped keep his teeth healthy, particularly the back teeth, where plaque piles up.

Buy a canine brush and toothpaste, but before you introduce brushing, prep your dog for four days by giving her teeth and gums a twice-daily rub with your index finger two days in a row. Introduce the toothbrush on the third day and the toothpaste on the fourth day. Check your dog's breath all the time. Doggy breath isn't always entirely sweet, but a horrible smell can indicate an abscessed tooth or a serious illness.

It's also vital to check your dogs eyes regularly. Be vigilant about bloodshot eyes, yellowed eyeballs or black dots that might appear on the eyeball. Some breeds, such as Pugs, also need to have their eyes cleaned of debris weekly. Cocker spaniels get tears in their eyes constantly, so their eyes tend to crust up. You'll need to clean that guck out regularly by gently pressing a face cloth moistened with lukewarm water over the dog's eyes for a few seconds to soften the crust before wiping it away.

By taking good care of your dog, you're not only ensuring that she'll have better health; you're also dedicating time, energy and attention to your dog that will enrich your bond of affection and respect. It's also another great way to build up trust and to help your dog accept your role as the alpha leader of your household pack. That way, she'll find it a lot easier to kick back and relax.

Recap: Coddled Canines

Dogs should be praised and rewarded for being our wonderful companions, but many serious anxieties, insecurities and aggressive behaviours result from dogs being overcoddled and treated like four-legged infants or surrogate partners. It's our duty to be responsible, caring and trusting caregivers to our dogs, but not coddlers. Infants don't have forty-two sharp teeth and the capacity to eat us for dinner. It's a no-brainer that our pooches can't possibly play the role of adult human because when dogs are used as replacement partners or friends, their own needs aren't being met. We ignore that fact at both species' peril. Here's a checklist of ways to ward off the dangers of overcoddled dog syndrome by using positive methods and products to maintain the health and happiness of our dogs:

* Never speak to your dog in a high-pitched tone
   (unless you're doing the ouch exercise from Chapter 6,

which trains a dog to respect boundaries by teaching him how to verbalize discomfort or pain).

* Never baby-talk to your dog. If you do, he'll see you as weak and in distress.
* Never let your dog go up on the human furniture— and especially not your bed. If you want to bond with your dog, get down on the floor.
* Don't humanize your dog by expecting her to fulfill your emotional needs.
* Patience-train your dog to curb insecurity and fear of being alone.
* Play hide-and-seek and other thinking games that stimulate your dog's mind.
* Be cautious about giving your dog behaviour-control medications before you've done everything you can to draw out your dog' s potential.
* Refrain from heavy petting with your dog. Give him an occasional massage instead.
* Show your dog you love her by meeting her need to be active, letting her experience all the sights, sounds and smells of the world.
* Don't shower your dog with expensive, useless and, in some cases, dangerous products. Invest in products that enrich your dog's life: three toys, healthy dog food and a few basic grooming aids.

Two's a Crowd

MULTI-DOG FAMILIES

MYTH: If your dog has behaviour issues, it's a good idea to get a second dog to keep the first one company.

REALITY CHECK: Bringing a second dog into your dog's life won't fix behaviour issues. It can be a recipe for total disaster, causing a pile-up of issues, challenges and stresses. It can actually heighten the potential that both dogs will be sent to a shelter, dumped in a ditch or euthanized.

Dogs Playing Poker

People think that when you leave two dogs home alone, they're going to break out the proverbial cards, poker chips and stogies. They often do, so to speak. Not literally, of course, but with badly behaved dogs, the mind games often start as soon as they hear the front door closing. I know this because

I often do an eye-opening experiment with my clients. We pretend we're leaving the house and even get in the car and drive down the street. Then we sneak back to observe the dogs. Well-adjusted dogs might play a little bit, but for the most part, they'll be sleeping.

With poorly adjusted dogs, though, it's a different matter altogether. If you have a badly behaved dog or an alpha dog who thinks she's the household CEO, she'll either teach the new dog her favourite negative behaviours or manipulate the other dog to do all sorts of naughty things to get him into trouble. The manipulating dog might be looking for a partner in crime or she might be a good dog who developed jealousy issues after the new dog arrived, much like an older child when a newborn comes home. But whatever the case, by adding a new dog to the household mix, you'll just be piling any existing issues up higher and higher and making it so much more challenging to curb negative behaviours. Dog owners also often underestimate the gravity of dog sibling conflicts, which can lead to deadly consequences.

Aggression in multiple-dog households is one of the most common topics brought up by people who email me about inter-dog aggression, and they often send crime scene photos that haunt me for weeks. It's typically very difficult for dog owners to pinpoint the true household troublemaker, and I can do so only after I've assessed each dog and, of course, also the human owners. Nine times out of ten, the humans have neglected to meet either of the dog's needs. There might be favouritism or the owners might simply believe that the dogs should be treated differently. This often happens with breed profiling or when people choose to treat their large dogs differently than small dogs. We often have to go back to square one and re-train every member of the household, sometimes doing all the exercises I've already discussed in this book, and most importantly, I need to make it clear to the Two Legs in the family that they absolutely must establish and maintain alpha positions to prevent one or all of their dogs from trying to overthrow their leaders.

The Case of Berta and Ernie

One of my clients called about a problem male dog causing destruction in the household through excessive barking and home-wrecking behaviours like digging. The family already had a two-year-old female dog, but they'd recently adopted a one-year-old male dog. Let's call the pair Berta and Ernie, after Bert and Ernie, those bickering roomies on *Sesame Street*. After working with the two dogs for a while, I realized that the male dog, Ernie, wasn't the problem at all. He sat and lay down on command over and over again, and he had the patience and submissiveness of an ideal dog. Berta, on the other hand, put on an act as if to say, "Oh, yeah, I can lie down for you." She did lie down twice, but the third time, all of a sudden, she went nuts and tried to bite me. She might as well have been saying, "Just forget it! I'm not lying down for anyone."

It was a real eye opener for the owners. They'd never, ever seen her act aggressively. After that incident, I believed that the female was actually "telling" the male to misbehave, but I wanted proof for the family. We left the two dogs in the back-yard and did the pretend-to-leave thing. Then we sneaked back into the house to observe the dogs from the kitchen window. Berta was lying on the deck, watching Ernie sniff around in the yard. When he looked at her, she stared him down for at least fifteen seconds. Then she got up and turned around, sitting with her back to him. Ernie started to bark, but Berta still kept her back to him, which made him bark even more. Then she stood up and approached him, staring at him intently the whole time. He stopped barking immediately and froze like a statue. Then Berta turned her back again and started to stroll back to the deck. Ernie immediately started to dig a hole in the garden, glancing up at her retreating backside periodically. When she got back to the deck, she lay down in the sunshine and relaxed, watching him as if to say, "Thanks for the entertainment." She had articulated nothing verbally but had used her body language strategically to manipulate him!

I've seen plenty of dog sibling interactions, and that episode would have gone very differently with a well-adjusted older dog who knows the rules and wants to teach the younger sibling to maintain household harmony. When Ernie started to bark, Berta should have said, "Hey, not acceptable behaviour. Cease and desist." Or she should at least have done something to acknowledge the other dog's attempt at communication. Dez did that a lot with Max during his first few months with us. If he barked for no apparent reason, she would give off a quick, loud, "calm down" bark.

Alpha dogs will often turn their backs on other dogs after disciplining them; it's the same silent treatment that can be so effective in human-dog relations—like putting a hockey player in the penalty box. But Berta was doing this while Ernie was busying himself with normal, acceptable doggy activities. By purposely turning her back, she was punishing him for doing something normal, and that caused his confusion. He barked as if to say, "Hey, what's the problem. And why are you ignoring me?" When Berta continued to ignore him, he notched up the barking to attempt a conversation: "Come on. Give me a clue here. What's the problem?" But Berta refused to engage Ernie or to show him the ropes about etiquette, and that is extremely manipulative.

If the human parents had been inside trying to enjoy some peace and quiet, they would simply have assumed that young Ernie was barking excessively, and they would then have yelled at him to cut it out, which is exactly what Berta wanted. But in this case, nobody stepped in, and the young male dog eventually stopped barking and went back to checking the daily newspaper. Berta then realized she had to turn the manipulation knob up to eleven. That's why she got up off the deck and approached Ernie as if to engage him but instead stared him down and turned her back again. Now Ernie was really confused. "What the heck's going on here? I was just checking the news. Why are you turning your back? This is so frustrating."

The male dog had a few options at that point. He could have gotten in her face and tried to engage her somehow, and that could have led to a fight. But he didn't. He'd probably tried that before and all it got him was trouble, either by the female disciplining him or the human parents stepping in to break up what they believed to be a fight that he'd picked. By now, Ernie clearly knew that Berta was the alpha. He'd been in a no-win situation for months, and the more he lost, the more control she gained.

So, feeling stressed and anxious, with no guidance that he could trust, Ernie started digging. Maybe he was just digging to relieve the internal tension or maybe he was literally searching for something, I'm not sure. Whatever the reason, it was clear that by going back up to the deck and lying down facing and watching him, Berta was condoning his bad behaviour—one that *she* had set in motion! She manipulated him into digging what could have been his own grave. If their parents hadn't witnessed this strange scene while being educated about typical dog sibling behaviour, they would have assumed he was up to his usual bag of rude, disrespectful tricks. They would have continued to say, "As *if*, Brad! She's such a good girl." But now it was glaringly apparent: Berta was the family alpha and wanted Ernie out.

When professionals advise people to get a second dog, the owners often take the attitude that the first dog will take care of the second dog and that the owners won't have too much work to do to give the dogs exercise and mental stimulation. The opposite is typically the case. When two dogs are left alone and the alpha of the pair doesn't acknowledge the owners as the household alphas, both dogs will be starved of their basic needs

The key focus for training Berta out of her sibling rivalry was to de-throne her and put her human owners in the lead positions. By putting her on umbilical, they could closely monitor her behaviours around her younger brother, and that also allowed her to bond with her owners, in case she'd been feeling neglected. It was imperative to get her socializing with other dogs, too, so she'd learn how to mix and she'd realize that you can be top dog and command all sorts of respect and admiration without resorting to manipulation and bitchiness. I also encouraged the owners to take each of the dogs out individually, so the pooches could get out of each other's hair for a while.

Berta took well to the training, and in the process, her owners realized that they had been slacking off on meeting her basic doggy needs for physical and mental stimulation. That's likely why she'd been taking her frustrations out on her new brother.

Sibling Rivals

Humans often underestimate the gravity of sibling dog conflicts. They'll say that on a scale of one to ten, the problem is about a six. But when I meet the dogs and see them interacting, I realize that the dog is scoring the problem at ten: serious business.

Well-trained dogs know that the humans are the leaders, and dogs are constantly negotiating their status with other dogs whenever they interact with each other. Rarely does any interaction between two well-balanced dogs result in really aggressive behaviours—so skin is rarely broken. But if you bring a new sibling into the life of a dog who already has behavioural issues, the aggression in dog play can become pretty nasty. If I'm dealing with sibling puppies from the same litter, the trouble becomes glaringly apparent at about two years and four months later, almost to the day. It usually starts long before that point in the form of subtle eye openers that people often choose to ignore: two dogs might clash over a bone or some food, for instance. But once the siblings hit the age of three, all hell can break loose as the jockeying for pack leadership position escalates.

Many of us have seen firsthand that human siblings often have conflicts, jealousy issues and territorial spats. Ditto for dogs, whether they're siblings from the same litter or unrelated but living in the same household. The conflicts might be as minor as barking or as major as biting.

Sometimes sibling dogs will team up and you simply have double the dose of bad behaviours to contend with. All of a sudden, you have two dogs pooling their individual doggy resources: two military tyrants under one roof, plotting a coup. Maybe the dog that came first has been eyeing the postie for a few years, drooling and barking and scratching, hoping to finally get a piece of him some day. "Oh, how will I ever get out and have a chance to sink my teeth into that interloper?" he's been thinking. Then another dog shows up and becomes assistant security guard. After all, what else is there to do every morning? They've now both thoroughly scoped the entire house for potential breaches and come up with nothing. Then, one morning, while Senior Dictator is taking her pre-postie nap, Dictator Junior is outside sniffing and digging around. Eureka! He finds some softer ground near one part of the fence. "Prison break!" he barks, and the other dog comes scurrying out of the doggy door. They hit the front yard just in time for the postie's arrival. It sounds like a weird cartoon, but I hear stories like that all the time.

At other times, siblings of different breeds—particularly one big dog and one small dog—are treated very differently. The big dog might sleep outside in a doghouse while the little dog cuddles up inside with owners that infantilize him, calling him their "baby" and giving him special treatment. Then they wonder why Big Dog doesn't take a shine to the little four-legged toy. This can lead to downright deadly behaviour, especially with dogs that have obsessesive tendencies around small animals. If Big Dog has such obsesssion issues, he'll start to fix those tendencies on Baby Dog. Then, one morning, Baby Dog heads outside to hang with Big Dog.

Maybe Baby Dog's being his typical yap-happy self, looking to play. Or maybe he's oblivious about how to play with other dogs because he spends so much time as a lap warmer. Maybe Baby Dog starts barking orders, trying to one-up Big Dog on the alpha meter. Maybe this offends Big Dog. Or maybe he reads this high-pitched yapping as a sign of weakness and pain and grabs the opportunity to take matters into his own hands, putting a stop to something that isn't right in his eyes.

Big Dog didn't wake up that morning with his sights set on murder, and perhaps he didn't even start the fight in the first place. Each dog battle is unique and complex, especially if you're dealing with a situation in which the owners have shirked their responsibility to take the lead role and provide effective training. But it's quite possible that the younger dog wouldn't come out alive from that backyard encounter.

When owners bring a new dog into their home, they must establish their two-legged leadership immediately, no matter what the ages of the current and new dogs. It's imperative to set up a consistent, disciplined training schedule for the new member of the family and be on the lookout for any subtle cues that a seemingly mellow dog is trying to manipulate the sibling into misbehaving. And, by the way, when it comes to conflicts with cohabiting dogs of different genders, I've noticed that females almost always score top dog, so it's wise to avoid stereotyping a female dog as being a member of the weaker sex.

Substitute Dog Teachers

As I mentioned earlier, adding a second dog to the family sometimes gives the owner a false belief that the first dog will take care of the second dog, giving the humans some time off from parenting. But to be a good dog tutor and mentor, your dog has to be mature, secure, balanced, well adjusted to being submissive among humans and well educated about the rules and boundaries. Is it a good idea to leave the four-year-old in charge of the toddler or infant? Of course not. Ditto for dogs.

If your dog has even a minor issue, like barking, she'll teach the other dog that bad behaviour. The so-called professionals will say that if one dog has a buddy to keep her company, her excessive barking, chewing or elimination problems will somehow disappear. That just doesn't happen, and even the most well-behaved sibling dogs can't possibly provide each other with all the mental and physical stimulation they need.

In response to that comment, people will sometimes say something like "Oh, but Harry and Sally have a big backyard for playing and frolicking." The size of the yard has nothing to do with it. It's like a sterile fish tank compared to the big, smelly, action-packed world over the fence. And now the dog has to share this tiny cell with another dog? They can't get out, let alone get away from each other. With domestic dogs, it's only the humans who can truly release them from their stifling and boring prison cells. Anything else is a weak substitute. Sure, dogs can have fun together, but I know firsthand that they aren't that thrilled about being stuck in the backyard, even when they have each other's company. The real fun starts when they can explore the big outside world together. Dez and Max, for instance, had their best times as a pair when they were off-leash, exploring the wilderness or a big city park. And on doggy daycare field trips with a bunch of other dogs, they were truly able to get back to their wild dog roots.

When I put surveillance cameras into clients' homes for the TV show, people are pretty shocked to find out that no doggy parties are going on unless you count manipulative game playing and home wrecking as parties. A well-balanced elder dog sibling who's more than three years old might help maintain order and establish rules and boundaries, but a younger dog wouldn't be able to do that, and a dog with behaviour issues of his own couldn't perform that function, no matter what his age. Whatever the age of the mature dog, human owners have to be extra-attentive to sibling rivalry issues and pay a lot of attention to all interactions between the dogs. Canines are intelligent, and they'll attempt to manipulate other dogs and us. They might even test our alpha status for their entire lives, so we can never give them the upper hand. They will naturally have to establish doggy rank, but it's our job to ensure that they have respect for our household rules.

Many people I know have no problems with multiple-dog households. But the humans who run those homes have to do their job to safeguard against all the problems I've discussed in this book. Some multiple-dog families have very active lifestyles. They're constantly on the go, and their dogs are typically a part of that stimulating mix. As long as the owners maintain alpha status, that situation gives their dogs the stimulation and guidance they need. Other multiple-dog owners are ranchers with a number of herding dogs who get the stimulation and work they crave, along with a lot of space to get away from each other when they want to do that.

When I'm called in to assist a multiple-dog family with training, at least half of the time, one of the household pooches wears the family crown and the other canines are duking it out for the throne. About 75 per cent of the time, one of the dogs is acting up or instigating another dog's rude behaviour. The one who's causing trouble might want to rule the roost or she might simply be unwilling to share her space because she's in her terrible twos (see Chapter 10) and needs re-training or she's entering her golden years and has trouble adapting to big life changes. Or she might just be a spoiled-rotten brat who refuses to play sharesies. She might also be noticing some favouritism going on among the Two Legs, especially if there are different rules for the other dog, which happens a lot when a cute pup joins the household and takes centre stage. We see it happen with humans: parents say they never play favourites, yet it happens anyway.

Love Is Blind

I get so many emails from people who continually bring new dogs and other pets into their families—and often these are "rescue pets" adopted from shelters or from family friends. In many cases, these owners will justify their actions by saying things like "You can never have too much love in your home." But nine times out of ten, the story veers off into nightmare territory: usually, one of the dogs has mauled another animal to death or has started lashing out at humans. Or I go into one of these homes and it's like a scene from *Animal House*— an accident waiting to happen. As I've said before, dogs don't perceive love and affection the way we view them, and when human owners don't meet their dogs' needs, the result is canine anxiety and aggression.

With multiple dogs, you *can* have too much of a good thing. The more caregiving you have to do, four-legged or two-legged, the more responsibilities you need to juggle, the more schedules you need to accommodate and the more unique personalities you need to satisfy. You can't just take one of your four kids to ballet class and soccer practice and tell the rest that they'll have to learn cello, gymnastics, hip hop dancing or whatever when they grow up. I know from doggy daycare that juggling the needs of more than half a dozen dogs is a full-time job for professionals. Owners of multiple dogs often have to rely on strict schedules just to get through the day, and by now, I'm sure you know how I feel about unvaried routines. So I urge you to think long and hard before you adopt any new pets if you already have a dog.

Mixed-Animal Families

Many families have no trouble living in multi-pet households. They have lots of happy stories and adorable snapshots of their dogs playing and bonding with other dogs, cats, rabbits or whatnot. Just the same, many dogs don't like being around other kinds of animals. Some haven't been socialized enough, and others don't get enough stimulation from being around a particular species. But for a fair number of canines, it's simply a matter of personal taste. My schnoodle, Rudy, has a particular lack of fondness for cats, and we respect that about him. If he has to hang with cats when we visit family and friends, we do our best to let him keep at a comfortable distance, but if he does take the offensive and lashes out at a cat, he will be corrected with a timeout. I've heard of dogs shredded by cats, but more often than not, the cat, or any other creature who's smaller than the dog, is the victim of these interspecies blowups, so do your best to prevent that from happening.

Get to know your dog's specific sensitivities to other creatures by watching how he reacts to a variety of situations, places, people and other animals before you even think about bringing another species into his life. To test him around other pets, go and hang out with a friend who has that type of pet and see how your dog reacts. To determine compatibility, don't do this once but a number of times. If your dog plays nicely, then be sure to educate yourself as much as possible about that other pet. But even if the two species get along, you should not add another pet to the household if you can't meet both your dog's needs and the needs of the other pet.

Recap: Multiple-Dog Families

We need to take sibling rivalries very seriously, especially if one or both of the dogs become aggressive. Here's my checklist for preventing sibling dog friction:

* Don't even think about adding a second dog to your household until your current dog is three years of age and has been exposed to a lot of socialization with other dogs.
* To effectively manage sibling rivalry issues, you will need to establish the lead household role and provide all of your dogs with basic training.
* Allow sibling dogs time apart—alone with you and with other dogs
* With problem dog behaviours, looks can be deceiving. Be watchful of any manipulation tactics that dogs might use to make the other dog act out.
* Treat all of your dogs like dogs. Don't let double standards and biases affect the way you treat each

individual pet.

* Don't get caught in a love-will-save-the-day mentality. There's not always enough love to go around for all of your pets.

* Be watchful of whether your dog(s) have anxiety issues or obsessive tendencies with small animals, and if so, don't bring other, small pets into your home.

CHAPTER NINE

Puppy Love

PUPPY MILLS, PET SHOPS OF HORRORS AND MY KEY METHODS FOR SUCCESSFUL PUPPY TRAINING

MYTH: A puppy is ready to join your pack whenever you are.

REALITY CHECK: A puppy needs at least eight weeks, ideally nine weeks, with his mother before you take over. Yet many breeders and pet stores hawk puppies who've been removed from the litter weeks earlier. This sets pups up for many negative behaviours and makes training and bonding much more challenging.

Rudy the Pocket-Sized Terror

Right now, Rudy the stellar Schnoodle, is curled up on his bed, spooning his little stuffed bunny. It's hard to believe that only four years ago, as a seven-week-old puppy, he was a little tyrant with an enormous mouth and attitude. Rudy was so manipulative and bull-headed at first that he even refused to be taken for a walk.

"Rudy was my first dog," says Daniela, his owner.

"I didn't grow up with dogs or know anything about them—especially that he should have been with his mom until he was at least eight weeks old. I had this little five-pound schnoodle, and he wouldn't walk. A dog that refuses to walk? I'd never heard of that, and I didn't have any idea what to do about it. Rudy would just put his butt down on the ground and flip me the bird. He had to control and dictate everything that happened. He was so resistant and refused to be managed."

I started working with Rudy and Daniela when the schnoodle was nine weeks old. Man, was that puppy a handful. Whenever you wanted him to do anything, he'd glare up at you as if to say, "Go take a hike. You have no idea who I am." Rudy exhibited so much bravado, but he also had separation anxiety issues because he'd been removed from the litter too early—so he'd whine and cry whenever Daniela left the room. He also had those tenacious schnauzer traits that can lead to some serious behaviour problems if the dog's not well trained. The two issues combined could have turned him into a featherweight thug. I shiver to think how bad it could have been if he'd also been treated like a lap dog and saddled with little-dog syndrome.

In this chapter, I'll discuss all the key steps you should take *before* you even start window shopping for a new pup, including learning as much as you can about the various practices of breeders, pet stores and shelters. The most important thing to know is that pups, as I've mentioned before, are often yanked from their dog moms before they're eight weeks old, and this causes many negative dog traits. I'll also talk about the need to proof *yourself* against the many negative *human* behaviours that are particularly tempting to indulge in with cute little pups: overcoddling, baby talking, carrying the pup everywhere. Owners might think they're showing love to their pets by doing these things, but such behaviours can actually lead to very serious and hard-to-fix dog misbehaviours. And no matter what the breed, size or temperament of your new pup, it's crucial to start training your puppy as soon as she enters your life, so she learns how to become a well-adjusted member of your family and an awesome dog citizen.

RESEARCH PUPS

*S*ix-week-old puppies still living with their moms and who've had little exposure to humans have been able to pick up human learning cues like pointing and gesturing.[45] This observation fits with the results of other research, which compared dog pups and wolf pups between three to five weeks of age. It was discovered that dog pups were better at social communication—such as vocalizing distress, tail wagging and gazing at people's faces—while wolf pups showed aggression and avoidance behaviours.[46]

Baby Love

During a pup's first weeks of life, he dines on mom's nutrient-packed milk. He also bonds with his mom and siblings and learns basic etiquette about play, socialization and the rules of conduct and engagement. And when he starts to explore a new environment, it's all done under his mom's watchful eye. These first weeks of pups' lives with their moms are precious and critical for their health and well-being.

To deny puppies all this bonding and learning experience is to set them up for failure. Almost every single pup I've ever met who was removed from the litter before eight weeks of age—sometimes just a few days shy—suffered negative consequences like separation anxiety and had inappropriate behaviours like home wrecking. These traits can often be fixed, but the required training takes a lot of time, effort and patience on the part of the human parent. Why put your pup and your family through that? Why rush the process?

I can't stress enough how important it is to do as much research as possible about the dog-eat-dog world of puppy mills and pet stores. Too often the adorable little creatures languishing in malls have been ripped away from their four-legged moms weeks before they should be, which often sets the little critter and his human owners up for a lifetime of hurt.

Some dogs are born messed up because of in-breeding and backyard breeding practices. They should be euthanized and put out of their misery, but instead they're passed off as regular puppies. The families who buy them are then sentenced to further grief. Most of problem dogs I meet are healthy, and though they've been removed from the litter too early, they can be trained to become happy, well-behaved dogs. But I've met at least a hundred dogs who couldn't be trained, no matter how dedicated the owners were to teaching their pup new ways. I implore you to take this issue seriously and not to be tempted to impulse-buy a puppy. Do your homework and find a good breeder.

———

Investigate Your Breeder

Some people spend more time shopping for stereos, cell phones and appliances than for a pup. When buying these everyday items, they'll read consumer reports and check the credentials of an individual or company, but they neglect to investigate the credentials of a breeder. That can be a downright fatal mistake in the long run. I've seen some nasty puppy mills, so it's imperative that you do your due diligence before you even think about getting a pup.

The best way to find a breeder is through friends and family with stellar pups of their own. If that's not an option, ask a few local vets or your co-workers or go to local dog parks and look for people with great pups and dogs. Of course, even then, you need to weigh the information you've received, but at least you'll be getting recommendations from satisfied owners. Some breeders have websites where you can find a lot of information about them and perhaps also gauge whether they seem to be in it just for the money. But beware of the cute shots of pups frolicking in a picture-perfect setting. You can't know whether they're a quality breeder unless you go to their location and see for yourself. But before you visit, call the prospective breeder and ask some important questions.

The first question you should ask is whether you can pick up your pup at nine weeks of age. The breeder should respond favourably, saying that's his or her typical *modus operandi*. If the breeder attempts to convince you that you can take your pup home earlier, say goodbye, hang up the phone and find another breeder.

Secondly, ask whether they breed different breeds, because if they do, they may just be in it for the money. Ask how many litters the bitch has had, the age of the bitch and when she started breeding. She shouldn't have had more than two litters by the age of four, and if it's her first litter, she should be at least two years old. Ask the breeder for references you can call—and make sure to call as many of those as possible. Talk to the breeder's vet as well, but remember that some vets are tied in to breeders and get a cut of their sales.

If you're all clear so far, book an appointment to visit the breeder. But arrive early. If you've booked your appointment for, say, Sunday at 1 p.m., go on Saturday at 10 a.m. instead. You'll catch them off-guard and you'll see what the environment looks like when they're not expecting you. Before you see the pups, ask to see the parents—especially the mother. She should have a clean, comfortable living arrangement and be able to come and go as she pleases. If she's separated from her litter, that's a bad sign. The adult dogs shouldn't appear fearful or have any negative behaviour traits. You could also ask for the pedigree of the parents and ask about any genetic illnesses that affect the specific breed.

Even if the breeding situation looks good, don't make a commitment that day. Go home and think about it for a few days before you make a decision. I know people who were sucked in to getting a pup *because* the breeder's environment was substandard. They set out to get a certain breed of pup, but they arrived at the breeder to discover dozens or hundreds of poor little dirty, whining, shivering pups in cold, filthy cages. Obviously, seeing puppies living in conditions like that will pluck at your heart strings and you'll feel the urge to rescue those poor little creatures and gallop off into the sunset together. Don't do it! Get yourself out of there immediately. Then call the SPCA and the Better Business Bureau right away and rat those bad breeders out.

Owning a dog is a huge responsibility, so please do the best you can to safeguard against bad breeders. By starting off with a pup that has been raised by his mom in a healthy environment for the right amount of time, you'll be setting both species up for success.

Pet Store Puppies

I highly recommend avoiding pet stores altogether. If you buy a pup from one of those outfits, you'll have no way to check the facility where the pups were bred, and you won't be able to meet the pups' first dog and human parents. Many pet store pups come from puppy mills, which means that these pups spent the first precious weeks of their lives enduring substandard care. The pet store might say that they don't buy pets from puppy mills and that all pups come from federally inspected facilities, but according to the Humane Society of the United States, that doesn't guarantee quality any more than possession of a driver's licence proves that the licensee is a safe driver.[47]

You really have no way of knowing when a pet store pup has been removed from the litter. Pet shop staffers might say that the puppy is eight weeks old, and that might be true, but many states and provinces in North America require that puppies be quarantined for up to two weeks before being sold, either direct to stores or to brokers who act as intermediaries for large pet store chains. During that period, there's often at least a few days of travel (sometimes in crowded trucks packed with rows of caged animals) before the pups arrive at the store. So if you do the math, it becomes obvious that an eight-week-old puppy in a pet store could have been removed from the litter before it was six weeks old.

A pet store's priority is to make money, and I'm a firm believer that you shouldn't leave a purchase as important as a dog to an industry that engages in these dubious and downright dangerous practices in the interests of profitability. What's the harm in waiting two to three weeks for the pup to bond appropriately with her mother and her litter and be weaned? I suspect that pet stores know that so many families window-shop for pups—especially families with small kids. So the smaller and cuddlier looking the dogs are, the more animals they can move out the door. In my mind, this is just another example of an industry-driven vicious circle that sets families up for a heap of heartache. Safeguard yourself against this by never setting foot in a pet store so you don't fall prey to impulse pet shopping.

Pups from Animal Shelters

I have mixed thoughts about shelters. On the one hand, I know so many great shelters whose managers and staff take seriously the responsibility of fostering dogs, and they are justifiably proud of that fact. They do a great job of assessing dogs, pinpointing behaviour problems and being watchful of anxiety issues. They provide their animals with proper nutrition, and they implement training programs to suit the dogs. They also do their best to tell the truth to prospective adoptive parents, so there are no surprises once a dog becomes part of a new household.

Unfortunately, however, many other shelters are much less truthful about problem dog behaviours. I've had to clean up a great deal of carnage because shelters haven't given families full information about problem dogs. I then have to help the owners cope with the very difficult decision of sending their dog back to the shelter. The problems begin when shelter staffers misrepresent a dog's characteristics. For instance, they might tell a family with children that a specific dog is great around kids, yet within days in the new family, the new pet bites a family member. Or they'll say that a particular dog is wonderful off-leash, but as soon as the family takes him to the park, he runs away.

My biggest pet peeve comes in the form of clients telling me that their newly adopted dog was beaten and abused by a previous owner. I hear this story over and over again. When a salesperson or shelter staffer tells tales like this, they might be able to guilt people into adopting a dog, but they're often unfairly saddling the dog and the new family with a history that may or may not be true. I understand all too well that shelters are trying to find homes for too many dogs crowded into too few shelters. But to lie to a family, especially one with children, or to convince them to adopt a problem dog can lead to downright deadly consequences. Where is the accountability?

The ugly truth that many shelters refuse to acknowledge is that not every dog is salvageable. Instead, they pass the dog on to a family. In many cases, the family then realizes the dog cannot be trained and they are left with the difficult decision to have their pet euthanized. That decision should have been made earlier by the shelter professionals—not left to families who are forced to hire dog trainers to sort through the wreckage and make this tough judgment call.

In our society, some animal shelters are no-kill shelters and others are kill shelters. At one time I worked near a no-kill shelter, and many of the dogs that were adopted out from that place should never have been sent to *any* home because they had severe behavioural issues and multiple aggressions.

No-kill shelters will say that no dog will die by their hands, but in my books, the apparent compassion in such statements smacks of self-righteousness and *lack* of humanity. These shelters are more than willing to send a dangerous dog to a great home, creating a scenario with potential for both physical and emotional hurt—and ultimately leaving the family to do the deed that the organization refused to do themselves. Approximately 40 per cent of my workload involves dogs who were adopted from shelters. One of these dogs had a track record of biting family members, but the shelter sent him back out *four times* without warning families about his aggression. Eventually, he bit a four-year-old in the face. The family then asked me to assess the dog, and I had to make the call to have him euthanized.

THE TOP TEN REASONS WHY PEOPLE SEND THEIR DOGS TO SHELTERS

* Moving
* The new landlord doesn't allow pets
* Too many pets in the household
* Maintenance costs
* Human personal problems
* Inadequate housing
* The owners couldn't find a home for the dog mom's pups
* The owner doesn't have enough time for the pet
* Pet illnesses
* Biting [48]

Bringing Puppy Home

Puppies are so darn cute that it's hard to resist overcoddling them. But I hope that by now you appreciate the many dangers of doing this. Nurturing and training your pup for success starts and ends with you. You are that dog's caregiver, so it's imperative that you check your human baggage before you even think about getting a pup. Once that wonderful bundle of energy comes home with you, your number one training assignment is to make sure your human emotions don't stand in the way of bringing up an emotionally and physically healthy dog. It's best to bond with pups by playing games like tug, which I talked about in Chapter 6.

Puppy training should start immediately. If you can't dedicate time and effort into providing the best possible pup parenting, don't get a puppy! Get one of those robot dogs. I've met plenty of people who say their vet told them that puppies don't need training before the age of one. And many say that puppies *can't* be trained before that age. Maybe these vets knew only inadequate trainers, but whatever the case, puppies do need training, and they can be trained, during their first year of life. That said, I don't recommend "puppy class." It sounds cute, right? Well, cute is not going to give you a well-behaved and well-balanced animal. Puppies learn best from older dogs. During their first weeks of life, for instance, pups spend most of their time sleeping and watching their mom, and they start following her around as their bodies strengthen. Then they keep on learning from their mom and from older dogs, which is why I never offer puppies-only classes. Instead, I mix them up with dogs of all ages and with my older, helper dogs.

Training should actually start as soon as you leave the breeder or the shelter. Follow all the rules I outlined earlier about being careful to use the right tone of voice, about avoiding heavy petting and about car safety. Here are the key things you should do before you even set foot in the house with your new pup:

* Leash your pup in the car, and once you get home, put her on the ground and let her check out the sights and smells of her new neighbourhood. Hang onto her leash, but give her leeway to do her own exploring. Don't carry the dog directly into the house.

* Make sure you're in the lead as you walk up the pathway and enter your home.

* Once you're inside, limit the number of rooms your pup can sniff around in, so she doesn't become over-whelmed. (As the days pass, you can introduce new rooms, leading the puppy in and giving her time to check out each one.)

* When it's time to eat, make sure you eat first.

* Don't let the puppy go up on your furniture and don't plunk her on your lap. Get down on the ground to play with her.

* It might be difficult to resist cuddling your cute and furry new friend, but restraining that urge and cud-dling only as on-the-ground play is actually the best gift of all.

* When playtime is over, introduce your pup to her bed or crate and say, "Bed" so she can start learning a verbal command.

* Get your puppy to lie down on her bed or in her crate and say, "Good buddy. Go to bed."

* Never let the pup sleep with you, but make sure that the pup's "bedroom" is in a warm, dry and comfort-

able spot. I also don't think that a pup's bed and sleeping area should be in your bedroom, but many people do that anyway. Rudy's crate was next to Daniela's bed. For the first month, the crate door was kept closed at night, but Rudy is a great sleeper, so Daniela started leaving the door open, and after a few months, Rudy graduated to his crab-shaped bed.

* When your friends come to meet the pup, ask that they refrain from gushing verbal hellos, baby talking and putting your pup on their lap. You might think it sounds ridiculous to lay down all of these rules, but you don't let guests come in and trash your house, so why should you let them handicap your awesome new pup?

It might be a good idea to put this list up on the fridge for the first few weeks as you become accustomed to having four new little paws in your household.

Rudy: Taming of the Schnoodle

Your puppy is going to do a whole lot of damage if you don't establish rules and boundaries immediately. To establish your alpha status, start with umbilical training right away, making sure that you're always in the lead when you walk your pup or when someone comes to the door.

This umbilical process was easier said than done with Rudy, the wild child. Luckily, he had an equally tenacious owner, who dedicated herself to training. At first, Rudy was so unwilling to move when Daniela tried to walk him that he wore his paws raw and she had to buy booties for him. Daniela and Rudy came to my group training classes at least twice a week, so Rudy was mixing with all sorts of other dogs. But it still took about two months before he would sit consistently on command or walk without pulling the leash.

"Rudy loved to party with other dogs, and he learned a lot from being with Dez and Max," says Daniela. "I didn't want to pamper my dog and give him little-dog syndrome, and with Rudy it was obvious from the start that if I wasn't providing strong leadership, he would never do what I told him to do. He needed to trust me and know that I could manage him safely." Daniela was able to take him to work with her during that critical period, so Rudy had very active days, mixing with all kinds of people. That helped take care of his separation anxiety issues, but he still needed to know how to get along on his own.

To prepare Rudy for independence, Daniela did the patience training I discussed in Chapter 7. It was important to show him that Daniela wasn't abandoning him every time she left the house but also that excessive barking wouldn't be permitted. "Consistency is such a key factor with patience training," says Daniela. "I was warned that schnauzers tend to be yappy dogs, and Rudy did whine a lot. I knew that if I didn't get control of that, it'd be very difficult to manage. I'd put him in the kennel, then take a few steps and as soon as he barked or whimpered, I'd say, "No noise." If he did it again, I'd give him a correction under the jaw. I had to be mindful to use the proper, firm intonation in my voice and make sure I had the time and patience for that exercise.

"Rudy can still be quite yappy. He likes to talk—sometimes more than I'm in the mood for. But it's important to let him use his voice. If he barks when someone comes to the condo, I say, 'Okay,' and then if he barks again, 'Leave it.'"

Rudy wasn't a home-wrecker, because he was taught that human possessions are off-limits, and whenever he tried to chew anything, Daniela would say, "Leave it" in a firm voice and replace the object with a rubber duck named Earl. Except for the odd roll of toilet paper, the teething process was pretty painless."

Expect accidents in this early stage, especially ones involving teething-related chewing. In Chapter 6, I gave advice about tug games and teaching your puppy to recognize and articulate that ouch means "steer clear." Daniela and Rudy did a ton of tug games, and after Rudy knew what ouch meant, Daniela taught him to relinquish anything in his mouth and prevent territorial aggressions with a similar process. She'd put her hand close to his mouth and then say, "Ouch" in a high-pitched tone, so it sounded as if she was in pain. Then Rudy would pull away, learning that any time a hand approached, he should keep a respectful distance.

Never forget that pups are born pack animals. From the first weeks, they are jockeying for food with their siblings, and no matter what the breed, they quickly learn their place in the dog pack—with their dog mom as leader. You'll see skirmishes among siblings fighting for food and attention, but these are simply challenges that pups quickly adapt to under their mom's ever-watchful guidance. If a pup steps out of line by being too hyper or too aggressive during play or around feeding, you'd better believe that mom will quickly step in and discipline him.

In the human pack, you have to take on the mother dog's disciplinarian role. If you neglect to show your pup that you're the boss, she'll quickly learn to become *your* boss.

It's a great idea to teach your dog the human rules during

playtime because this builds up the pup's trust, confidence and agility skills. But don't go overboard. Pups are wired for sound and can easily become overstimulated. Also make sure you give your pup some time on her own. That way, she'll learn to appreciate downtimes, and she won't become co-dependent.

Also be sure to expose your puppy to other dogs at the dog park and help her burn her wonderful pup energy by giving her a lot of exercise in a variety of locations. Avoid the routine rut by mixing up your feeding, walking and bedtime schedules.

House Training

Start house training first thing in the morning. Here are the basic steps:

* Take your pup outside on the leash.
* As you guide him to a designated relief zone, keep the leash slack and give him some time to smell the ground en route to make the trip as pleasant as possible.
* Say, "Go" in a calm, assertive voice. Your dog will probably pee first and then sniff around for a while before pooping, so don't rush him! Stress can make it difficult for humans to finish their business, and it's the same for dogs.
* After he's finished, praise him verbally or with a chest scrunch.
* Do the same after his next meal and again before you head for bed.
* Keep an elimination journal as well, as I discussed in Chapter 6.

★ Be watchful of your pup's behaviour while you're house training. When they need to go, some pups bark, some go to the door and some just gaze at you, hoping you'll get the message. When Rudy needed to go for a bathroom break, his voice became kind of squeaky. You should also start training your pup to control his bladder and bowels. As I pointed out in Chapter 2, doing umbilical training is a great way to do this.

There are going to be accidents during the early training stage. To prevent that problem, it could be tempting to put those diaper-like puppy pads on her, but I don't recommend it. All they teach your dog is to believe that things that feel like these pads—especially rugs, pillows and clothing—are really good bathrooms. As I mentioned in Chapter 6, most dogs can hold their bladders through the night, but you should still allow for accidents to happen, especially if you're away from home for long stretches of time. If these elimination issues continue, however—whether they happened two minutes ago or two days ago—you must take the pup to task. Leash her up and guide her back to the spillage. Then tell her in a calm, firm tone that this is a no-no. Then make a point of ignoring your pup for at least fifteen minutes while you do whatever you want to do. Don't talk to her or acknowledge her presence. That way, she'll realize that her actions have consequences.

Puppy Pre-School

Teaching your pup how to follow your lead and your commands to sit, stay, come and stop are key to fostering a well-behaved dog that you can trust to celebrate life with, whenever and wherever. When it comes to dog safety, the world is a giant booby trap, rigged with a mind-boggling variety of dangerous and potentially deadly situations. Do your best to minimize the dangers by teaching your pup to sit, stay, come and stop (see Chapter 4). Then, once your pup has these skills, you can start off-leash training. This training will safeguard your pup, it will provide the mental stimulation that pups and dogs crave and it will build your pup's confidence, dexterity and ability to be independent, yet under control.

Doing umbilical training with your pup teaches the rules of the human pack through movement—in *his* language. Once your pup is following your lead and the leash is nice and relaxed, you'll be ready to give him the off-leash test at the dog park. If you're not completely confident, find a fenced tennis or basketball court. Keep the pup leashed up but drop the lead and let it drag on the ground. Then start walking. The dog should follow right beside you. Then start changing directions. When you do that, your dog should still follow your lead. Keep repeating the exercise, changing up your directions all the time. If your pup continues to follow you, praise her physically. But all of this is just a prelude to the best reward of all: teaching your pup the basic commands that will allow her to go off-leash safely. (See Chapter 5 for the exercises.)

Murphy, a yellow Lab client of mine, was off-leash-trained within four months. But other dogs will take longer. The length of the process depends not only on the dog's character but also on the commitment and patience of the human parents. Rudy took about eight months to off-leash-train, but he had a very dedicated parent, my guidance and the help of other stellar dogs. It's important not to push the doggy envelope too much while you're training. If you or your dog start to become frustrated, take a good break and have some fun together.

As I've said before, mix training in with your daily activities, whether it's doing sit-stay en route to the video store or doing patience training while you grab a coffee. I hope that by now you appreciate that any routines can have a negative impact on your dog. People have busy schedules, so they'll tend to train at a certain time of day, such as after work. But your pup will probably be excited to see you after being home alone all day. In that case, it's best to go for a romp first and then finish up with some training. And what if your pup responds better in the morning, just like some morning people? Don't get stuck in a training routine that's so strict you're fostering inflexibility and limiting her potential.

"The first time we did off-leash street training, I felt like I was going to throw up," Daniela admits. "But I knew that I needed to trust Rudy, and to do that, I had to be confident. Otherwise, I'd fail him. Now he can go hiking on all sorts of challenging terrain. I never think he can't do something. He rode a Sea-Doo this summer and has a little life-jacket for swimming."

Puppy Personality

At six months, your puppy's unique personality will start to shine through. But often that's about the time that owners' interests and attention start to wane. Kids can be especially fickle, so don't let them slack off on their pack responsibilities. Kids have to do household chores, and caring for the dog should be one of them. If your children start losing interest in playing with the growing pup, sit them down and ask them why they're no longer playing with him as much. Get their feedback and try to make them understand that the dog is missing out on the bonding time he needs. Ask them how they would feel if their siblings or friends suddenly stopped wanting to hang out with them. The goal is not to guilt-trip them into submission but to get them to empathize with the dog, so they'll want to restore and foster that amazing bond.

Same goes for us adults. Sometimes we think we're well beyond those negative playground or high school cliquey behaviours. But too often, like socially immature kids and teenagers, we drop good relationships just because they don't seem so "cool" anymore. So make sure you don't start slacking off on your responsibility to chaperone your maturing pup and foster his unique character. Consistent training is key in the first year of your pup's life. And playtime is a critical and wonderful way to bond with your dog throughout his life. After your pup turns one, you'll really see the doggy gifts start to come.

Recap: Puppy Love

Bringing a puppy into your life is a sixteen-year or longer commitment. Do your best to set your puppy up for a healthy, happy life by choosing one that's had at least eight, ideally nine, weeks to bond with her dog family. Then, once your pup is home, provide her with the tools she needs to become a well-adjusted dog. Here's a checklist:

* Never buy your pup from a pet store.
* Investigate the breeder extensively before you make any commitment
* If you choose to adopt, be aware that some shelters might provide you with incorrect information about

your chosen pup.

* Establish your alpha status as soon as your pup sets foot in your home. Put your pup on umbilical so he learns to follow your lead during your initial bonding.

* Teach your pup what's off limits and what's within bounds by interrupting any of his attempts to home-wreck and by providing him with three or fewer toys.

* Allow for accidents to happen with elimination and with teething-related chewing. But if these problems persist, discipline your puppy with a leash correction or a timeout.

* Do basic sit, stay, come and stop training so your pup will be safe outdoors.

* Don't coddle or baby-talk to your pup, and don't treat her like a lap warmer. Spoil your pup with a steady dose of exercise and a mixed bag of environments, so both of you can discover what your pup likes to do best.

* Make sure your pup starts socializing with other pups asap, so that he knows how to mix and bond with other dogs.

CHAPTER TEN

Evolutionary Training and Bonding

U nlike the case with books, there's no such thing as a final wrap party when it comes to dog training. Sure, you should celebrate your team's successes, but these are building blocks for a relationship that should grow and morph into an even stronger bond over the years. A good relationship is always a work in progress, so it's imperative, and also really fun, to continue to pay attention to and learn from your dog as she matures and evolves.

Anticipate that problem behaviours might develop as time goes on, necessitating re-training. But never let that discourage you! These phases will pass as long as we provide consistent leadership. We also need to acknowledge whether our actions, or our neglect of our dog's basic needs, contributed to these behaviours. Use these little road bumps as an opportunity to do a refresher course with your dog. I encourage dog owners always to stay a few steps ahead of their dogs by working little training sessions into their daily activities.

The Terrible Twos

We've all seen little humans in the terrible twos phase: the meltdowns, the tantrums, the stubbornness and manipulation. Dogs hit their own terrible twos phase at about seven to ten months of age. Here's what happens: She used to come and now she doesn't. He used to respect boundaries; now he trashes the house. Don't be alarmed when this happens. All it means is that your pooch is going through an important growth period, and it will last for only about four weeks. Some dogs purposely push the boundaries to see what they can get away with. Others are simply saying, "Remind me again, please."

All the same, you'll need even greater consistency and patience to hang in with your dog when she's going through the terrible twos. You'll likely have to give her a refresher course on many things she's already learned. Don't try to introduce new stuff to the agenda; just plug away at the basics. Then, after about a month, your dog will almost always get back into the rhythm again. One of the most important things to do during this critical period is to give your dog proper interruption and correction. You might have to develop a new correction method, and you'll have to use interrupting techniques to prevent any negative behaviour. With Dez, I'd say, "*Demona*"—in that strict tone that parents use to show their kids they're stepping out of line. You could also introduce a new hand signal or a timeout. It's also a great idea to re-introduce umbilical and agility exercises. They're an excellent aid for minimizing any emerging negative traits and for reinforcing that important bond between you and your dog.

Mid-Life Crises

Between five and seven years of age and between seven and nine years of age, your dog might also hit another speed bump. These phases are something like a human mid-life crisis, except that instead of getting a sports car, the dog all of a sudden reverts to chewing, not coming when he's called or trashing the living-room couch. To counteract the negative trend, introduce some new stimuli into your dog's life by trying a new activity, such as rollerblading or boating. Go to new dog parks so your dog has the opportunity to make new friends.

Make sure you address any behavioural issues as early as possible. If you don't, your dog will often start to become aggressive by the age of nine, seemingly out of the blue—and when dogs do this, they typically lash out at their owner. The change will appear to be dramatic and unprecedented, but chances are, that dog will have been sending out subtler warning signs for a few years as if to say, "Hey, I'm getting bored with the routine. I need some new form of stimulation." Maybe your own lifestyle has changed. For instance, you might be travelling more often or you might have started a new job. Great for you, but if you're giving your dog less time and slacking on your commitments, she'll naturally rebel.

TEACHING AN OLD DOG
THE SAME OLD TRICKS

*P*ups and mid-lifers aren't the only ones with behaviour issues. Elderly dogs can have them too. But that doesn't mean that senior canine citizens have to keep on

going downhill. According to researchers at the University of
Pennsylvania's School of Veterinary Medicine, aging pooches
with common problems like destructiveness, elimination dif-
ficulties, barking and separation anxiety do benefit from re-
training. [49]

Dogs in Their Golden Years

Elderly dogs aged ten or more are especially vulnerable to
developing behavioural issues. Even if a dog has been well
behaved for years, when he hits the decade mark, he might
turn into a home wrecker or he might develop elimination
problems or become aggressive. Health issues sometimes play
a part, especially if the dog has mobility-related illnesses like
arthritis or blindness. But sometimes these issues arise simply
because an elderly dog isn't getting enough moderate daily
physical and mental exercise.

Elderly dogs should be celebrated and respected for their
wisdom and experience. Dez had no behavioural problems
in her senior years and she lived to the ripe old age of
twenty-two. But I didn't slack off on my responsibilities to
her, even while I was mourning Max's death. That means I
didn't heap my grief onto her shoulders either. I appreciated
her golden years and the wisdom she had developed as an
amazing dog citizen.

Dez had been physically strong and mentally sharp all her
life. She'd always been such an active dog and a tough nut.
But, naturally, she was much more fragile in her last few years.
Her weight had dropped from a healthy forty-five pounds
(about 17 kilograms) to thirty-seven pounds (about 20 kilograms)—not a good number for a Border collie–Australian

shepherd cross. Her coat was still healthy and fluffy, but looks can be deceiving. Underneath, she was much more delicate, but she still needed to get outside to walk and pick up the daily news. Remembering those lazy walks of ours puts a smile on my face. A dog walk that might have taken a minute or two now took twelve minutes, but of course, I didn't rush her. Dez had always been there for me, and I wanted to be there for her when she needed me most. Those leisurely walks also allowed me to slow down and smell the roses *with* her. That was a really precious time. I treasured these golden years with Dez and the experience gave me a greater respect for all seniors, whatever the species.

Older dogs might not be able to handle the outdoor activities of their youth, but you can replace some of that physical exercise with stimulating indoor games and less demanding outdoor recreation. Dogs can't enroll in Spanish class or pull up a chair and tuck into a crossword puzzle, but they can play mentally stimulating indoor games like hide-and-seek, and they can engage in low-impact outdoor activities like walks and fetch games. It might take a little longer to engage your older dog in such activities, so give him some extra time to get into play mode.

I strongly believe that you *can* teach an old dog new tricks, but try not to introduce too many changes into a geriatric dog's life. Some of my clients bring a new pet into the home when their dog enters the golden years, but as I pointed out earlier, if your current dog has any behaviour issues, adding another one can cause trouble for the entire household. I suggest that you hold off on getting a new puppy unless your well-adjusted elderly dog is still spry and agile, in which case, it may not be a bad idea. But ask a veterinarian to check your dog's health before you contemplate adding a second canine to the mix.

An elderly dog needs your guidance and attention just as much as a puppy—perhaps even more. So to keep your senior dog engaged, I highly recommend getting into basic dog re-training exercises, including doing umbilical in the house and on walks. You might also have to give your dog a refresher course about the rules and boundaries you've always set. Most importantly, give your dog the gift of your time, so you can enjoy the last years of your dog's life.

Raising the Bar on Human-Dog Relations

The sky's the limit when it comes to the many ways we can bond with our dogs and keep them physically and men-tally stimulated throughout their lives. As you come to understand what your dog likes best—swimming, playing fetch, hunting, herding, hanging with other dogs or mel-lowing out in the sun—try to provide her with the activ-ities she craves most of all. But don't become too complacent about these activities because you'll then get stuck in a routine rut. Try new things, like rollerblading or rock climbing with your dog or going on a boat if your dog is physically and mentally agile enough to do these things. If your dog can handle it, push the envelope to give your dog a nice surprise now and again. You can also give your dog a new leash on life by sending him to daycare or by hiring a dog walker once in a while. With continued time and effort, you can both try new things and celebrate life successes together.

———

Back Where We Started: The Checklist of Doggy Needs

Let's go back to a dog's basic needs one more time. Use this as a checklist for making sure you continue to meet your dog's needs as he or she matures, so your bond continues to grow. And remember that these are only basic needs. Of course, it's also important to be attentive to your dog to discover other legitimate needs and then to meet them.

* Maintain your alpha status consistently throughout your dog's entire life. Interrupt and correct any negative behaviours so your dog has a clear understanding of rules and boundaries.
* Learn to speak in your dog's language: movement. Teach your dog skills through non-verbal commands. Refrain from baby talking and from speaking in high-pitched tones.
* Avoid treat training. Instead, buy yourself a bag of patience so you can actually teach your dog the rules of life.
* Provide your dog with a mixed bag of exercise, including time at dog parks, so she can socialize with other dogs.
* Reward your dog by learning to off-leash-train her, so she has the ultimate reward: freedom.
* Play games with your dog that stimulate her need to flex that muscle between the ears.
* Be a responsible caregiver by being sensitive to how changes in the environment—a new pack member, a new home, holiday festivities and new pets—affect your dog.
* Never humanize your dog by showering him with

human affection, letting him hang out on the human furniture or buying him expensive and useless props. Refrain from saddling your dog with your own human baggage.

* Avoid strict routines. Such routines stifle dogs and make them inflexible to sudden changes, such as dog-free vacations, business trips and new additions to your family.

* Get to know your dog's unique character. Be sensitive to, and patient about, the fact that some dogs learn rules and skills more quickly than others.

* Be aware that negative behaviours might emerge throughout your dog's life, necessitating re-training. Use that time to strengthen your bond and to introduce new stimuli.

* Celebrate your life with your dog!

Epilogue

I don't know about you, but I'm much better with actions than words. But it's important to me to get my message out in as many forms as possible, so I hope that with this book, I'll be able to teach even more dog owners to live the happiest life possible with their dogs. I sincerely hope that I've given you some good ideas about human-dog relations and that I've motivated you to take actions to enhance your relationships with your dogs. All the same, this book certainly isn't meant to be a "written-in-stone" bible of interspecies communication. I don't pretend to know how to read dogs' minds and I don't pretend that my words are from God. Every pooch is different, and we limit and stifle our canines by standardizing any training. Like humans, dogs are not robots that can be computer-programmed. They're unique and wonderful creatures who deserve to be celebrated as individuals.

I consider myself incredibly fortunate to be called on to help people understand and appreciate their individual dogs, and I'm honoured that many people have not only lent me their ears but also invited me into their lives and helped me take my dog training methods and my life to higher levels. I feel truly blessed that I've had so much happiness and success in my life so far. I've worked hard, but all the blood, sweat and tears have been more than worth it. I expect many more challenges ahead—in fact, I thrive on them and I think dogs do too. We can't expect perfection from our dogs any more than we should expect it from humans, and besides, perfection is a total bore. We *will* make mistakes. There will be frustrations that push our patience. There will be heartaches too. But I think the greatest gifts of all come when we put ourselves on the line and are vulnerable. If I hadn't had such amazing relationships with my dogs, I wouldn't have had to mourn their passing, but I would have missed out on so much of the best things in life. I certainly wouldn't be the person I am today.

We will fall on our faces sometimes, but I think it's better to suffer these temporary burns and pick ourselves up, with the helping hands (and paws) of those who motivate us and bring out our best qualities.

Dogs have picked me up and encouraged me to push the limits so many times already, and I know I'll learn so much more from them—and from dogs and people that I've yet to meet. I feel that my life education is just beginning because I know that I'm a work in progress and there's so much more to learn. Right now, I'm excited about getting off my butt and continuing that process. I hope you feel the same way as you finish reading this book. And thanks for listening.

Talk is great, but when it comes to dogs, it's cheap. So if you have a dog, or want to have one, I hope you'll start applying the approaches I've described in these pages sooner than later. And through it all, I wish you and your phenomenal dog companions all the best that life has to offer. Onward and upward!

NOTES

1. P. Savolainen et al., "Genetic Evidence for an East Asian Origin of Domestic Dogs," *Science* (November 2002): 1610–13.
2. J. Topál, Á. Miklósi and V. Csányi, "Dog-Human Relationship Affects Problem Solving Behavior in the Dog," *Anthrozoos*, 10 no. 4 (1997): 214–24; Monique A. R. Udell and C.D. L. Wynne, "A Review of Domestic Dogs' (Canis Familiaris) Human-like Behaviors: Or Why Behavior Analysts Should Stop Worrying and Love their Dogs," *Journal of the Experimental Analysis of Behavior* (March 2008): 247–61.
3. Darcy F. Morey, "Burying Key Evidence: The Social Bond between Dogs and People," *Journal of Archaeological Science* 33. (February 2006): 158–75.
4. Udell and Wynne, "Domestic Dogs' Human-like Behaviors," 247–61.
5. Kerstin Lindblad-Toh et al., "Genome Sequence, Comparative Analysis and Haplotype Structure of the Domestic Dog," *Nature* (December 2005): 803–19.
6. Dog Genome Sequencing Project: http://www.broad.mit.edu/node/343.
7. Á. Miklósi, J. Topál and V. Csányi, "Comparative Social Cognition: What Can Dogs Teach Us?" *Animal Behaviour* 67 (2004): 995–1004.
8. The Family Dog Project: http://etologia.aitia.hu/main.php?folderID= 896&articleID=3930&ctag=articlelist&iid=1.
9. Topál, Miklósi and Csányi, "Dog-Human Relationship," 214–24; Udell and Wynne, "Domestic Dogs' Human-like Behaviors," 247–61.
10. Deborah L. Wells, "Domestic Dogs and Human Health: An Overview," *British Journal of Health Psychology* 12 no. 1 (February 2007): 145–56.
11. Research from the Center for the Human-Animal Bond, Purdue University: http://www.vet.purdue.edu/chab/.
12. Á. Miklósi, J. Topál and V. Csányi, "Big Thoughts in Small Brains? Dogs as a Model for Understanding Human Social Cognition," *Neuroreport* (March 2007): 467–71.
13. The Humane Society of the United States: http://www.hsus.org/pets/issues_affecting_our_pets/pet_overpopula-tion_and_ownership_statistics/the_crisis_of_pet_overpopulation.html.
14. *Ibid.*
15. Humane Society of the United States: http://www.hsus.org/pets/animal_shelters/common_questions_about_animal_shelters_and_animal_control.html.
16. The National Council on Pet Population Study and Policy (NCPPSP) Survey, 1994–2006: http://www.americananimalwelfare.com/over-population.html
17. The Family Dog Project: http://etologia.aitia.hu/main.php?folderID= 896&articleID=3929&ctag=articlelist&iid=1.

18. Topál, Miklósi and Csányi, "Dog-Human Relationship," 214–24; Udell and Wynne, "Domestic Dogs' Human-like Behaviors," 247–61.

19. Lilla Tóth, Mórta Gácsi, Joózsef Topál and Adam Miklósi, "Playing Styles and Possible Causative Factors in Dogs' Behaviour When Playing with Humans," *Applied Animal Behaviour Science* 114 (2008): 473–84.

20. Z. Horváth, A. Dóka and A. Miklósi, "Affiliative and Disciplinary Behavior of Human Handlers during Play with their Dog Affects Cortisol Concentrations in Opposite Directions," *Hormones and Behavior* (June 2008): 107–14.

21. C. Molnár, F. Kaplan, P. Roy, F. Pachet, P. Pongrácz, A. Dóka and A. Miklósi, "Classification of Dog Barks: A Machine Learning Approach," *Animal Cognition* (July 2008): 389–400.

22. A.P. Rossi and C. Ades, "A Dog at the Keyboard: Using Arbitrary Signs to Communicate Requests," *Animal Cognition* (April 2008): 329–38.

23. The Clever Dog Lab: http://www.nc.univie.ac.at/index.php?id=14571.

24. C. Schwab and L. Huber, "Obey or Not Obey? Dogs (Canis familiaris) Behave Differently in Response to Attentional States of Their Owners," *Journal of Comparative Psychology* 20 (August 2006): 169–75.

25. A. Leuscher and I. Reisner, "Canine Aggression Toward Familiar People," *Veterinary Clinics of North America: Small Animal Practice* 38 (2008): 1107–1130.

26. Topál, Miklósi and Csányi, "Dog-Human Relationship," 214–24; Udell and Wynne, "Review of Domestic Dogs'."

27. Udell and Wynne, "Review of Domestic Dogs'," 247–61.

28. S. G. Brown and R. E. Rhodes, "Relationships among Dog Ownership and Leisure-Time Walking in Western Canadian Adults," *American Journal of Preventive Medicine* 30 (February 2006): 131–36.

29. H. Cutt, B. Giles-Corti and M. Knuiman, "Encouraging Physical Activity through Dog Walking: Why Don't Some Owners Walk with Their Dog?" *Preventive Medicine* 36 (February 2008): 120–26

30. A. L. Podberscek and J. A. Serpell, "Aggressive Behaviour in English Cocker Spaniels and the Personality of Their Owners," *The Veterinary Record* 141 (July 1997): 73–76

31. D. L. Appleby, J. W. Bradshaw and R.A. Casey, "Relationship between Aggressive and Avoidance Behaviour by Dogs and Their Experience in the First Six Months of Life," *The Veterinary Record* 150 (April 2002): 434–38.

32. A. Horowitz, "Attention to Attention in Domestic Dog (Canis familiaris) Dyadic Play," *Animal Cognition* 12 (August 2008).

33. J. Kaminski, J. Call and J. Fischer, "Word Learning in a Domestic Dog: Evidence for 'Fast Mapping,'" *Science* 304 (June 2004): 1682–83.

34. B. Hare and M. Tomasello, "Human-Like Social Skills in Dogs?" Trends

in *Cognitive Science* 9 (September 2005): 463–64.

35. E. A. McCrave, "Diagnostic Criteria for Separation Anxiety in the Dog," *Veterinary Clinics of North America: Small Animal Practice* 70 (March 1991): 247–55.

36. G. Flannigan and N. H. Dodman, "Risk Factors and Behaviors Associated with Separation Anxiety in Dogs," *Journal of the American Veterinary Medical Association* 219 (August 2001): 460–66.

37. Y. Takeuchi et al., "Differences in Background and Outcome of Three Behavior Problems of Dogs," *Applied Animal Behaviour Science* 70 (January 2001): 297–308.

38. C. J. Hewson et al., "Efficacy of Clomipramine in the Treatment of Canine Compulsive Disorder," *Journal of the American Veterinary Medical Association* 213 (December 1998): 1760–66.

39. Judit Vas et al., "Measuring Attention Deficit and Activity in Dogs: A New Application and Validation of a Human ADHD Questionnaire," *Applied Animal Behaviour Science* 103 (June 2006): 105–117.

40. http://www.fda.gov/cder/drug/antidepressants/anti-depressants_MG_2007.pdf.

41. Udell and Wynne, "Review of Domestic Dogs'," 247–61.

42. N. Endenburg and B. W. Knol, "Behavioural, Household and Social Problems Associated with Companion Animals: Opinions of Owners and Non-Owners," *Veterinary Quarterly* 16 (July 1994). 130–4

43. L.M. Freeman et al., "Disease Prevalence among Dogs and Cats in the United States and Australia and Proportions of Dogs and Cats That Receive Therapeutic Diets or Dietary Supplements," *Journal of the American Veterinary Medical Association* 229 (August 2006): 531–34.

44. D. P. Laflamme, "Nutrition for Aging Cats and Dogs and the Importance of Body Condition," *Veterinary Clinics of North America: Small Animal Practice* 35 (May 2005): 713–42.

45. Juliane Kaminski of the Max Planck Institute for Evolutionary Anthropology, quoted in Julia Koch, "Canine Smarts," *Spiegel*, July 9, 2007.

46. M. Gácsi et al., "Species-Specific Differences and Similarities in the Behavior of Hand-Raised Dog and Wolf Pups in Social Situations with Humans," *Developmental Psychobiology* 47 (September 2005): 111–22.

47. The Humane Society of the United States, "Pet Store Doublespeak," http://www.stoppuppymills.org/pet_store_doublespeak.html.

48. The National Council on Pet Population Study and Policy (NCPPSP) Survey, 1994–2006: http://www.americananimalwelfare.com/overpopulation.html.

49. B. L. Chapman and V.L. Voith, "Behavioral Problems in Old Dogs: 26 Cases," *Journal of the American Veterinary Medical Association* 231 (March 1990): 944–46.

BRAD PATTISON is an animal trainer and a human-being life coach who has been professionally remedying problem dog behaviour for over fifteen years. Best known for his TV series, *At the End of My Leash*, Pattison also founded Vancouver's Yuppy Puppy Dog Day Care Inc., pioneered the first Street Safety training program for dogs and facilitates courses that certify other dog trainers. His Six Legs to Fitness workout program for owners and their dogs has been featured on Discovery Channel's *Daily Planet*. During the Hurricane Katrina disaster, Pattison mobilized friends and created the Pattison Canine Rescue Team, which spent several weeks in Louisiana rescuing dogs from the floods. He lives in Kelowna, British Columbia.